Praise for
Please God, Send Me a Husband

"Readers will find a wealth of practical wisdom here as well as an energizing pep talk." *Please God, Send Me A Husband* is "a useful, sometimes inspiring guide to finding Mr. Right."

— *Kirkus Reviews*

"Dr. Monique Rainford-Bourne offers easy-to-read advice directed at women seeking marriage. Her light tone, quick chapters, and many examples make *Please God, Send Me A Husband* an intriguing and enjoyable read for those looking for romantic guidance."

"Overall, *Please God, Send Me a Husband* is a light, enjoyable read that offers something for anyone currently going through this phase of their life. More serious and thoughtful than most daring advice books, while also maintaining brevity and lightness, the work is a perfect combination from an educated, friendly author."

— *Foreword Reviews*

"While Rainford-Bourne's advice is from the Christian viewpoint, and backed by Scripture, the book is not dogmatic. Instead she discusses many of the relationship issues prevalent today such as living together, premarital sex, and divorce in a non-judgmental fashion."

— *Bluelnk Review*

Please God
SEND ME A HUSBAND

Heartfelt advice on finding Mr. Right from a woman who has lived it

MONIQUE RAINFORD-BOURNE M.D.

Whittingham House
Maryland

ISBN: 978-0-9864316-2-3

Published by Whittingham House, Maryland
Edited by Evette Porter
Cover design by Stewart Williams
Interior book design by Neil Fairclough
Printed in the United States of America

DEDICATION

This book is dedicated to my parents, Milton and Kathleen Rainford, for teaching me what a happy marriage is like, and to my husband Ryan for showing me what the "right man" is like. To my beloved Auntie Monica (God rest her wonderful soul) for choosing to confide in her niece, and for promising me that when I met him, it would be "Sooo good!" – and my husband, Ryan, for proving her right. To my son, my dear sweet Zane: if you do decide to get married one day, I hope that you will be the very best husband you can be and that God will place you with a woman who is worthy of you. And last, but by no means least, to my beautiful daughter Kia: my girl whom I knew was coming even before my positive pregnancy test, it is my prayer that if you choose to marry one day, God will give you the patience to wait for His choice and to be confident and prepared for the journey. As a mother, I hope that He won't make you wait *too long.*

CONTENTS

$\mathcal{A}$CKNOWLEDGEMENTS

As with my first edition, I cannot begin this book without thanking all those brave, wonderful, open, honest and courageous women, who shared their stories with me. Some even relived the emotional pain and suffering of failed relationships, so that other women could learn the lessons necessary to find love and happiness, and enjoy the kind of lives they so richly deserve. I cannot thank them enough.

I have a number of people to thank whom I can call by name. My special thanks to Marilyn Ricketts, who despite her professional role in reviewing the first draft of this book, took a personal interest and went above and beyond the call of duty. My girlfriends, the wonderful women who helped me realize some of the joys of being single, and a few of whom pored over this book to help me improve it.

My special thanks to my dear friends Vee (Venessa Martin Benjamin), Sho (Sha-Shana Crichton), Sofie (Sofia Samuels), Jacky (Dr. Jacqueline Duncan-Stines), Racky (Dr. Raquel Gibson-Onyonyor), and Kara (Kara-Sue Sweeney, my personal trainer who has been so much more) for poring over drafts and providing me with invaluable commentary that helped me improve the book. I need to make special mention of Jenny (Jennifer Lechuga). I actually did not even meet Jenny in person until after she reviewed the book. She was recommended by my dear friend Terri (Dr. Teresa Stone). However, Jenny's review was thorough, detailed and also extremely helpful in allowing me to fine tune this book to the version that you will read.

I would like to thank a number of other people who provided resources and valuable input — my hairstylist for a number of years, Adolf Raynor; my dear friend, Wendy Birthwright; my lifelong friends Camille (Lee) Chin and Alex Lee; one of my besties from college and even now, Dr. Andrea

Isaacs-Banton; my sister-in-law Shauna Bourne Di-Bella, my "baby" brother, Ryan Rainford; my older brother, Norman Rainford; my inspiring father, Milton Rainford; my amazing mom, Kathleen Rainford; and my loving husband, Chester Ryan Bourne. Last, but not least, I would like to thank my professional team including my friend Dean Clarke, who shot the beautiful cover for the first edition; Stewart Williams for the fresh creativity he brought to the cover of my second edition; Neil Fairclough, who brought the artistic side to my manuscript; Adrienne Sparks for her expertise in preparing the back cover copy and last but my no means least, Evette Porter, my editor. Her wisdom and experience forced me to push my boundaries to develop my book from a snack to what I hope will be for you a satisfying meal.

It is my hope that after reading this book, you will be armed with the tools to allow the right man into your life and ultimately get a husband. Hopefully, near the end of a long, happy marriage you will have the optimism and faith to say to a discouraged, single woman that when she meets the right man, it will be "soooooo good!"

*I*NTRODUCTION

"Confidence in what we hope for and assurance
about what we do not see."
Hebrew 11:1 Holy Bible, *New International Version*

It was 2005, and I was well into my thirties. I was tired — tired of being single, tired of being lonely and tired of disappointments. Here I was an established obstetrician and gynecologist. Professionally, I had worked hard, made a lot of sacrifices, and by many standards would be considered successful. But I was still single and alone. In my work, I spent plenty of hours counseling, seemingly happily married women and couples, about the steps to achieve a successful pregnancy. I walked them through their pregnancy, but despite my hopes I could not share in that kind of fulfillment. I encouraged single women through their painful dating experiences or their frustration at being single, silently knowing that I totally understood and felt their pain, frustration and loneliness. Yes, it was disappointing.

Over the years, it was difficult at times to even meet someone whom I found interesting, or if I did meet someone whom I found interesting, the feeling was not mutual. At times, I met men with whom I shared a mutual attraction, but after getting to know them better, I realized they were more talk than substance or that they were afraid of commitment.

It wasn't always the case that there was something wrong with them. I recognized that sometimes I was just attracted to men who were wrong for me. I knew it, but I ignored the warning signs. We were just not compatible enough to build a lasting relationship. At other times really nice men expressed interest in me but I just was not attracted to them and I could not find or force the attraction. I had a burning desire to be married, but the right man just was not coming my way.

Why was God making me wait so long? Why did he even put some of these bad choices in my path? Where was the right one? Surely, God had a reason for allowing me to go through through this misery. Certainly there were other women who were experiencing some of the same frustrations — women, like me, who believed that God had called them to marriage, but were wondering if His will was perhaps misguided because marriage had so far eluded us. Some stood by, even as they witnessed their close friends' marriages and the births of their married friends' children, and felt cheated by love.

Back then, I felt like I'd had it. I decided to make a list — a list of the criteria that I wanted in a husband. I was very specific — even listing how tall I wanted him to be: "Taller than me in heels," although I never specified how high the heels should be. I knew what I wanted in a husband because I was educated and prepared. I was educated by my many conversations with women and men over the years and by my own dating experiences. I was prepared because I had at least learned from some of my mistakes. Now, I realize that I was not cheated, and certainly not by God. All He was telling me was to wait. It was not the time. Either I, or my husband-to-be, was not ready for marriage.

As I grew older, I was practically convinced that God was not listening, or that He did not hear me. Although my faith had taught me otherwise, my belief was constantly challenged, and that maybe He had ignored the relationship part. But He never leaves out any part. Some of us are destined to be single and others are meant to be married. Either way, I pray that each of you receives God's guidance and has the peace of mind that comes from knowing God has a plan for you. However, if you are like me and are convinced that you are called to marriage, but doubtful because of years of disappointments

— continue to have faith and pray for patience. Indeed, He hears you and He is listening. Every one of your prayers has been heard. As I had been told by an aunt of mine, God is not only preparing you, but He is also preparing your mate. You may think you are ready for marriage, but he — your future husband — may not be quite there.

Perhaps my biggest regrets during the years that I was single is that I failed to appreciate the journey as much as I should have, and that I did not put my complete trust in Him and failed to realize that He would deliver right on time. In spite of my doubts, I had some remarkable experiences that I will remember for a lifetime. I went white-water rafting, downhill skiing, took Spanish lessons in Costa Rica. I witnessed Michael Jordan play basketball and shook hands with other sports celebrities. I developed interests and hobbies like ballroom dancing that to this day I absolutely love, and met friends that I will always treasure — friendships that have stood the test of time. Those friends helped me survive some dark days and made good days shine — friendships that because I was single made it easier to cultivate and grow — and that have continued to nurture me in my married life. However, the search for a mate and the success of finding him, or perhaps being open enough for him to find me, has led me to write this book. I hope this book will help you to not only find and choose the right mate, but to enjoy the journey.

In writing this book, I interviewed more than fifty women. I talked with many of them by telephone, some by Facebook and others were kind enough to complete questionnaires that I devised. Some of the women I knew, while others I never met and perhaps may never meet. Some of the women were single, some divorced, some married for only a few years and some married for more than sixty years. They were women of different races, religions and cultures. Some married their partners despite great obstacles and still prevailed, while other women were not so fortunate. Some women had never married yet still wanted to, and others had given up their quest for happily ever after. They answered very personal questions. I asked the married women how they met their husbands, whether or not they were "in love" then and even now. I asked them about the ups and downs of their marriage. I asked them if they would make the same choice again. I asked divorced women about their feelings for their husbands when they first got married and why they left. I asked single women if they thought they had missed out on opportunities for marriage. I asked virgins why they were waiting for marriage and non-virgins why they didn't wait. That was only the tip of the iceberg. I heard stories of fulfillment and happiness and others filled with regret. Some revealed hardships, while others enjoyed pleasure and contentment. However, all of their stories were useful in helping me write this book.

I have tried to describe their experiences as they were told to me, and I have changed all their names to maintain their privacy. I called on my own personal experiences and borrowed from my years of counseling hundreds of women over many years of being an Ob/Gyn. I supplemented my own research and expanded my knowledge by pursuing postgraduate education in psychology. I knew I would never have all the answers, but I wanted to have as many as possible.

Despite the struggles, I have always believed in the institution of marriage. During my single years, I remember reading about escalating divorce rates. I'd often asked myself why some marriages did not last and others did. At a particularly difficult time in my single life, I remember talking to my aunt, Auntie Monica, a few months before she died of cancer. She was in remission and was optimistic about life. She had been married to my uncle for more than forty years at the time. She described how her husband, my uncle, had pursued her. They were married after only a six-month courtship. She didn't tell me that she'd fallen madly in love, even if she had. She didn't tell me how romantic the courtship was, even if it had been a fairytale. What she told me was that he expressed his interest in her and she went with the flow. Years later, she told me that if he were to pass away before she did, that she had no desire to marry any other man. She had been satisfied with her life partner.

What she taught me in that conversation was to be open. The right man may not sweep you off your feet like in the movies, but he may be more right for you than someone who does. She taught me that I did not have to rush into or control the process, something I had a tendency to do with my type-A personality. Rather I should allow it to happen naturally, which was the case when the right relationship with the right man, who became my husband, eventually came along.

She also told me something in my last visit with her. At the time, I was struggling with whether or not I would be able to identify the right relationship. She told me that when I met the right person, it would be "sooo good!" She was right. When I met my husband, I felt a certain peace that I had not experienced in my past dating relationships. I did not wonder about his motives or his affection for me. His motives were entirely clear. He wanted me to be his wife. He did not play games or try to hide his feelings. And within a year we were married. Auntie Monica taught me that the right man would be better for me than any man with whom I had had a relationship with that had failed or any man that I had yearned for a relationship with but that did not materialize. The right man, my husband Ryan, most certainly is.

My husband Ryan and I have been married for more than eight years now. It hasn't always been perfect and we have had our disagreements, but I am confident when I say that we are happy. We both feel that we made the right choice in each other. Neither of us ever believed that we were each other's *only* choice, just the *right* choice. Ryan allows me to be me and supports me in my dreams. I sometimes think of him as the wind beneath my wings. He is one of God's greatest gifts to me.

I am so grateful for what I have. My husband was worth the wait. My two children were worth the wait. The road was not easy and because of that and despite all my imperfections, despite all the things I considered lacking in my life, I can easily thank God daily for all He has given me.

1

Are you sure you want to get married?

When I was in my late-20s and early-30s, I became more and more frustrated about not finding Mr. Right. At the time, I would ask older, single women why they had never married. I'd ask women who had been divorced, why their marriages had ended. I recall a friend accused me of being rude and insensitive. I didn't mean to be impolite, but it was my way of educating myself. I was sure I wanted to get married and I was sure that I wanted my marriage to work. I had heard stories and seen movies where couples fell out of love, and I did not understand it.

So the first question is: Are you sure marriage is your calling? Or in the words of my former parish priests, is it "your vocation"? Perhaps the best way to decide is through prayer and knowing yourself.

Sometimes we may choose to do something because we think it is the "right" thing to do. But we are all unique individuals, and what works for one person may not be best for you. Regardless of the pressures and expectations of family and society, at the end of the day, I will borrow this often used but certainly tried and true adage: "To thine own self be true."

Don't decide to get married because it suits someone else, whether it's your parents, your friends or even your boyfriend. Search your soul and rely on God to help you find the answer. Know that He will lead you to the best option for you. Mother Teresa lived a remarkable life. I am convinced that she lived the life that God had called her to, a life devoted to serving God as a nun, which meant she vowed never to marry.

Oprah Winfrey has done and continues to do great things in her life. Although she has been blessed with a life partner, she has chosen to forego marriage and children of her own. I suspect that it was not an easy decision, but based on how she has lived her life so far and how she continues to live her life, she made the right choice.

One of my former parish priest revealed to us at Mass one morning that before he entered the priesthood, he had a good job and was considering marriage with the boss's daughter, a woman he loved and had been dating. His boss — and prospective father in-law — even supported their marriage. But God called him to a different life. No doubt it must have been a tough decision at the time. However, Father Howard has been able to look back and recognize that it was the right decision.

If you believe, however, that God has called you to marriage, don't let the naysayers get you down. Don't listen to comments like "all the good men are gone" or "what if you never get married." Continue to live your life according to God's will, and be confident in His promise. After all, isn't that what faith is all about?

2

Are you really ready for love?

Years before I got married, I got some advice. I will sum it up in a few words: *Fix yourself first.*

If you want to attract the right man, be your best self — or certainly as close to it as possible. I am not suggesting that you have to have it all together when you meet him or even that he has to. However, if you have deep-seated issues in your life, you should make every effort to resolve them. If you can't do it by yourself, then consider therapy. This was the dilemma faced by a friend of mine, Mia.

Mia was in her early thirties. She was friendly, outgoing and had an interesting and challenging career, but she was always struggling with her weight. She readily admitted that she often sabotaged her relationships, despite the fact that she very much wanted to get married. She believed that the reason for this self-sabotaging behavior, which involved mentally checking-out of a relationship at the slightest hint of discord and staunchly maintaining her independence, was because of her lack of self-esteem. She struggled with her body image and that left her feeling that no one truly desired her as she was. Despite her insecurities, she yearned for companionship and the opportunity to share her life with someone.

If you can identify with Mia's story, take the time to be proactive about understanding and healing yourself so that you have a positive self-image both physically and mentally, even if it means psychotherapy. If you can't love and accept yourself, why should anyone else? If there are things you dislike about yourself, work on changing them. If you are convinced that you can't change them, then learn to accept them. Marriage is not an escape from your problems, and many women who use it for that purpose live to regret it. Realize the value in being single — and use it to your benefit. While you are still single, get to know and understand yourself better. Being single gives you the freedom to put your needs first. It gives you time to develop friendships with others. This preparation will strengthen your resolve and confidence and reveal whether your desire to get married is well-founded. It can also increase your self-confidence so that you can avoid those relationship traps.

For some, therapy might be too expensive. So what else can you do? Consider getting involved in your local church or religious group. This may afford you the opportunity to meet like-minded people, who can also be a source of strength and support. However, one size does not fit all. Investigate the group or church before committing wholeheartedly. The wrong group of people can also do more harm than good. Consider other social organizations — sororities, book clubs, or meet-up groups that share your passions — that may be better suited to your interests and personality. Participating in group activities can provide entertainment and companionship, and may lead to lasting friendships or personal relationships. It was during my single years that I signed up for ballroom dancing classes. I went to the classes on my own, since no partner was required. I just loved it. I performed in concerts and competitions I also had time to participate in a number of group activities including biking and hiking. I was also able to more actively participate in my church. All these activities allowed me to cultivate friendships that I still have to this day almost twenty years later. If there is something you yearn to do, this is the time to do it.

Many women, who have successful relationships, reinforced this message: you have to love and respect yourself first before anyone else can. And perhaps the best advice is that you have to have a strong sense of who you are — in other words, you should first know yourself.

Love yourself first

Stacey met Shane when she was only twelve years old. They grew up together in Brooklyn, New York. They went from friends to childhood sweethearts, according to Stacey as she fondly recalls the sweet boy Shane used to be. When he was sixteen, his parents divorced and it was then that Stacey began noticing a change in his behavior. Nevertheless, she ignored it. She held on to the image of how he used to be. She lost herself in him and focused her efforts on trying to help him to succeed at the expense of her own success and well-being. Her love for him bordered on "idolatry" and he became her entire world. She became pregnant with their first child at nineteen. Despite a tumultuous relationship and against her better judgment, she married him at age twenty-two, when she was pregnant with their second child. She was trying to do the "right thing" as a Christian woman. She tolerated his infidelity. She tolerated his lies and empty promises. She tolerated a man who was absent as a father. Stacey stayed in the relationship, despite the fact that it was affecting her health. It was even affecting the one relationship that she tried to maintain above all others — her relationship with God. She eventually divorced Shane.

Although, their marriage did not last, Stacey realized an important lesson: she learned to love herself first.

She admitted that when she'd heard the advice about the need for self-love and self-knowledge before marriage, she did not take it seriously. But experience taught her otherwise. It is "very true to love yourself first and understand who you really are, then you will be able to know what you really deserve." Stacey gained great insight into her relationship that will be discussed later.

Harvard psychologist Dr. Holly Parker sums up the importance of self-awareness nicely when she says "the most important relationship you will have is the one with yourself... and the most overlooked."

Independent women

Many of the women — both single and married — felt it was important to have a career and to be financially self-sufficient before marriage. I loved Destiny's Child popular song "Independent Women" and the catchy lyrics, which to me capture the spirit of what it is to be self-sufficient.

Cassandra was only twenty-one years old. She was a beautiful, but naïve young woman from a small European country. She travelled to London for a job opportunity and to escape her controlling and abusive father. One night she went to a party with some friends where she met William, a handsome man with a gentle manner, nothing like her father. She started dating him, and it was not long before he proposed to her. Still, she had her doubts. Initially, she didn't accept his proposal. Yes, she loved him. And after the third time, she said yes, even though it had only been a year since they had first met. Cassandra and William have been married for forty-six years. The unfortunate part is that she has always been unhappy in her marriage. One of the reasons that she stayed in an unhappy marriage was that she lacked financial independence. She candidly admitted that she had used her marriage to escape a controlling and abusive father. Basically, she left one bad relationship for another. Although there was no physical abuse, her husband was still controlling. She regrets that she did not have the opportunity to discover who she was and establish a career before she got married. She strongly believes that women should be financially independent in relationships. And she readily admits that she probably would have left the relationship, and still would, if she could afford to. She wasn't really ready for marriage. But at the time, her circumstances led her to believe that she did not have a choice.

It is important to underscore the necessity of self-awareness and preparation. It cannot be underestimated how significant these factors are in determining if you are really ready for marriage, and even more of a key factor in selecting the "right mate." Whatever it is that needs building in your life, work on it while you are single. Avoid waiting in a holding pattern until Mr. Right comes along.

By working to improve yourself, you will be better able to distinguish what you think you want in a husband, versus what you really need. It will also help you identify those qualities that are really important in a mate when he comes along, and help you recognize and avoid the wolves in sheep's clothing.

Wear your game face

Even if you have never played poker, you are probably familiar with the expression poker face. Essentially, that means even if you think you're losing in a relationship, don't let him know it. Recognize when it's time to hold 'em and when to fold 'em. It's a good strategy to have as you navigate the dating world. If a relationship isn't going well, don't stick it out for the sake of staying in the relationship. Ideally, you should have enough faith in your decision-making to believe that you will find and marry the right man, so that you won't need to bluff your way through a relationship. Meaning, if the relationship is going well, you will know if it's good to stay. And if it's going badly, you will accept that you may need to leave. Even so, there may be times when you feel less than hopeful. You may find yourself staying in a relationship against your better judgment. Try to share your concerns with close friends or family for moral support. Continue to pray to God for guidance. But try to not reveal your emotional struggles indiscriminately. They might be misread. Being vulnerable with the wrong person can make you fall victim to men who only have their self-interest in mind.

What is the ideal age to marry?
Some married women believe that you should get

married when you are older rather than younger. But there is no "right" age to get married. Based on my interviews, it is clear that one size (or age) does not fit everyone. One woman I interviewed named Olivia married when she was only twenty-two. And forty-one years later, she is still happy and very much in love with her husband. Another woman, Jenny, who has been happily married for thirty-seven years, was only twenty-three when she married. She attributes her marital success to the fact that she was very much her own person, despite having lived a sheltered life. Others, who married at a relatively young age were not as successful. Some women, even those who waited until their late thirties to marry, have not always enjoyed success. I don't believe that there is a "right" age to get married. If you strongly believe God is calling you to marriage, trust that He knows when it is the appropriate time.

How many men should you date first?

There is no magic number of dates or relationships

that you should have before getting married. The decision should be based on knowing yourself and your priorities.

Angela had always been popular with guys. Not only was she well on her way to achieving a professional degree, but she never had a problem getting dates. By age twenty-five, she had already fallen in love and suffered the pain of having the man she loved walk away. Now, she was engaged to a man, who she thought was going to be her husband. She certainly wasn't looking for anyone that summer day when she saw Duane at a barbecue. She instantly recognized him as her real life partner. Her relationship experience had taught her that.

On the other hand, Marci did not have that love-at-first-sight certainty when she met and eventually married Harold. He was the only man she had ever dated. Yet despite having had little dating experience, she enjoyed a happy, fifty-seven-year marriage that ended when he died.

How long should you date before marriage?
One of the trickiest questions is — how long do you need to date someone before marriage? Angela

was right in her choice of Duane, marrying him only seven months after their first meeting. And yet Olivia dated her husband for three years and Jenny for seven years, and all have had long, happy marriages. Some women are able to make a wise choice in just a few months. But for others, even after many years in a relationship, their marriage leads to divorce. In truth, there is no ideal length of time to date someone to insure a successful marriage. It has more to do with the two people involved.

So, I ask the question again: Are you ready for love? Or more specifically, are you ready to be married? First, be honest with yourself. More importantly, allow God to guide you. Rushing into anything will likely yield more harm than good. You will likely cause pain to yourself and in matters of love you will likely cause a lot of pain to someone else, too.

3

Do you know what you are looking for?

A few months before I met my husband, I started keeping a journal, which included a list of things I wanted in a mate. I had not kept a journal for years, so this was unusual at that time. But I felt motivated and inspired, hence the list. I was very specific about what I wanted and I offered up the list as a prayer. Within about one month of dating Ryan, I knew he was the *right man*. I was able to quickly realize it, because I had given a lot of thought and prayer to what I wanted.

In searching for the *right man*, I believe that it is important to establish your priorities. By that I mean, decide what qualities you want in your mate.

The criteria can take the form of a written list or coming up with a way to evaluate those things that are important in a mate: whether it is good looks, his financial status, his level of education, his interests, his faith, where he lives, where he is from, whether or not he wants kids and how many. Your list has two important functions: to recognize the right man when he comes along and to recognize the wrong man, because he's just as likely to come along too.

In making your list, be honest with yourself about who you really are. Sometimes, the things we think we want are not necessarily what we need. For example, a high-powered, woman executive might think that she needs an equally high-powered mate. However, the match might lead to a clash of egos and her being with someone who cannot accept a successful woman and who sees her as competition. Of course, if you have already taken the time to know yourself and resolve your issues, the list will be much easier.

Even with the list, Mr. Right might not meet every single criterion on the list. One of my younger and very wise cousins, who is happily married, recommends that you identify those things that you will not, and more importantly, should not compromise. It is important, even if you do develop a list, that you are flexible enough to make compromises in choosing a mate. Once again, the key is to be clear about what you can compromise on, and what you will not compromise on.

Only you can decide the best criteria for choosing your mate, here are some recommendations from women whose choice in partners have led to successful marriages and others who have learned from their mistakes.

Marry someone you have a lot in common with

It is a familiar adage: opposites attract. But women with successful and happy marriages often acknowledge that their compatibility with their spouses helped their marriages succeed. Similar interests, religious beliefs, backgrounds and values can be part of the glue that makes a happy marriage. While all of these qualities need not be shared, too many differences in background and personality can become a wedge in a marriage that contributes to its failure and unhappiness.

Ryan and I certainly do not have everything in common. He is an avid scuba diver. And although I learned to scuba dive when we were dating, I could really take it or leave it (more leave it). I love ballroom dancing, and even though he offered to learn while we were dating I have long accepted that I will have to partner with instructors if I want to continue ballroom dancing, much like I did before we were married. However, there is a long list of things we have in common, including our taste in food, furniture, houses, home decorating, (some movies) and even people we gravitate to as friends. This has made a lot of our decisions easier and requiring minimal compromise.

Look for someone that you can laugh with

Sally married her husband when she was only twenty-five, having dated him since the age of eighteen. Even after thirty years of marriage, she and her husband have been exceptionally happy. One of the most important reasons for the success of her relationship, she says, was that she married someone who she has fun and laughs with on a regular basis. Their shared easy-going humor helped them to more fully enjoy their life experiences, including raising their three children.

My husband Ryan told me he was funny soon after we met. I immediately thought that is something I should decide but I must admit, he does have a good sense of humor. And although I still find some of his jokes corny, he has provided many a good laugh for me. I am happier for that.

Like him for the person he is, not the person you want him to be

It may seem obvious, but women sometimes fall madly in love with men who make them feel on top of the world when they are with them, but who they may otherwise dislike. You may not like how he treats other people or friends and family. Maybe there are aspects of his personality that don't mesh well with yours. When the romance fades you may be left with a person that you no longer enjoy being around or someone who does not get along with your family or friends. This can be a major source of marital friction and can isolate you from friends and family.

I remember dating a guy whose behavior was unpredictable. I couldn't decide whether he was even a nice guy or not. If you have to think too hard about whether the guy you are dating is Jekyll or Hyde, then that should be a wake-up call. There's no point in marrying someone you think is a jerk or whose personality you can't be sure of day-to-day. Rest assured, there really are nice guys out there.

Find that person who you enjoy hanging out with even when you're doing nothing

If the relationship is based entirely on the exciting or expensive places he takes you to, you will likely become bored once the initial excitement is over.

Make sure that you spend time with him doing more everyday activities.

Tiffany and her second husband Conrad always take exciting trips together. They fly to other cities just to take in a concert. But Tiffany also enjoys time just hanging out together at home doing nothing in particular. She finds his company satisfying, with or without the glitz.

Choose someone who is more in love with you

Admittedly, the idea that it is good for one person in the relationship to be more in love than the other is debatable. However, you should be absolutely certain of the love of the man you choose to be your mate. Most of the women I spoke to, who had successful, long-term marriages, described their husband as the pursuer.

When Jessica first met her husband, George, she was seventeen-years-old. She was indifferent towards him. However, on the same day they met, George told his friends that he had met his future wife. She did not see him again for another three years, and during that time her feelings had not warmed. Nevertheless, by the time they got married, six years later, she had fallen in love with him. Forty-five years later, they are still happily married.

Marry someone who allows you to be you

Before I met my husband, a male friend of mine suggested that maybe I needed to tone down my personality to attract a mate. He believed that I was a little too intense and that the way that I approached life and relationships would be too much for most men to handle. I had frequently heard that men were intimidated by strong, professional women. And I did encounter some men, who seemed intimidated by my success and acted as though they were in competition with me. Ryan was totally different. Not only did I feel comfortable being myself with him, but I didn't have to tone down or change my personality. I felt supported then as I do now by my husband, and see the pride that my husband feels when I succeed.

You are who you are. No one is perfect. Everyone has flaws, but you deserve someone who not only lets you be who you are, but accepts and loves you the way you are. That does not imply that they love our every flaw but they love us enough to tolerate and accept them. Don't settle for someone whose love for you is based on how they think you should be.

To thine own self be true
My religion and faith in God has always been an important part of my life. Ironically, during my dating years, I dated an atheist. He had some good qualities, but it was always a fundamental difference between us. I thought maybe he would change or that I could convince him of my way of thinking, but that never happened. We eventually parted ways. However, during our relationship, I knew I was guilty of trying to make him fit into a certain mold rather than acknowledge that he was not the right fit. In your quest for a mate, be certain of those characteristics and values that are non-negotiable in a partner, and only consider those men who possess those qualities. Trying to

develop and maintain a relationship with someone who does not meet your criteria is doomed to fail.

Many of the women I interviewed said their Christian faith was important for the success of their relationship. Interfaith marriages or marrying someone who does not believe in God may work for some people. But if the very idea of being with someone who does not share your faith makes you uncomfortable, it probably won't work for you.

Do you like what you see?
Let's just say that I am biased. I honestly think that my husband is really handsome. In some of his pictures he reminds me of my favorite superhero character, Super Man, played by the late-actor, Christopher Reeves. Before I met him, I had always valued 'good looks' in a partner. Some might even say that I placed too much of a premium on looks. When I was still looking for Mr. Right, a male friend suggested that I consider dating more average-looking guys. I won't share my exact response, but let's just say I disagreed with him. The

bottom line is: physical attraction is important in our choice of partners. While there may be some consensus in what women find appealing in men, usually attractiveness is more a matter of individual taste. Of course, you will meet men who are intellectually stimulating, but it may be irrelevant if at the end of the day you don't "feel" it. If you don't feel it, don't force it.

Do your best and let God do the rest

Even if you decide to make a list of the criteria for choosing a husband, as I did, or you carefully consider what type of man best suits you, ultimately God is in control. Let Him guide you in determining the kind of man who is best for you, and let Him lead you even if it means throwing the list away.

4

Are you waiting in vain for his love?

Many years ago I met Leah, a smart, articulate, attractive woman, who ultimately became a friend. She was about fifteen to twenty years older than me. She had never been married, and I asked her why? She said that she had been in a long-term relationship for ten years that ended badly after she discovered he was unfaithful and dishonest throughout the relationship. After that relationship ended, she was deeply hurt and retreated from the dating scene for about fifteen years. By the time she was ready for a relationship and marriage, she was older and had difficulty finding a partner, partly because she found it hard to trust men even if they were worthy of her trust. Her past relationship had undermined her confidence in men.

But Leah's story is not unique. When I hear stories like hers, I find them heartbreaking. A woman full of hope meets a man, falls in love and puts her trust in him. She embarks on the relationship full of dreams about the future they will share together. She may spend years in relationships like this, only to realize that after giving him the space to become the man he wants to be there's no space left for her in the relationship. For some, the relationship ends unhappily. Sometimes the relationship's end is triggered by his dishonesty or infidelity, or he breaks it off abruptly leaving her to pick up the pieces and start over again. The worst part is she may have wasted years waiting on a man who was never going to commit. For some, those years may mean giving up the possibility of bearing children, or passing up opportunities to find true love. Add to that the painful reality that the future she'd dreamed of for so long was just that... a dream.

Cassie met Jonathon in the prime of her life. He was more

than twenty years older, confident, successful and wise. When she met him, she had already graduated from college, had a good job and she was establishing herself as an independent young woman. She was not interested at first, but Jonathon came on strong. She knew he was married, but he said he was separated. Supposedly, his wife was in another country and he had no plans of returning to her. Since he spent so much time with Cassie, she was not concerned that he would reunite with his wife. They went everywhere together. They took great vacations. She loved him and she loved the time they spent together. Then she got pregnant. But he stayed with her and was very supportive of their child. Several years into their relationship, he announced that he was going back to his wife. She was a single, unwed mother.

The relationship has been over for years now, but Cassie is still single. She maintains that her relationship with Jonathon sabotaged her opportunity to meet a potential husband and it still does. One of her fears is that their child will wittingly or unwittingly give Jonathon information about any man she is dating. The long-term affair she had has given her an unrealistic view of relationships.

Jonathon was willing to maintain the relationship, but only on his terms; she was always going to be the other woman and never the wife. I have heard both stories many times before and in many different versions. Sometimes, like Leah, women naively believe they are in a trusting relationship, only to have that trust abused and that innocence stolen. Like Cassie, some women can be seduced by someone promising much more than they ever expected, but under false pretenses. Other women may become trapped in long-term relationships with someone, even though they know it doesn't feel right — sometimes out of fear of being alone or insecurity about finding someone else.

Choosing a man who is unavailable — whether he is married, commitment phobic or maybe because the two of you are incompatible — is self-sabotage if you want to get married. Some women realize that their choices are unsuitable as mates. Yet they remain in bad relations, sometimes throughout their prime reproductive years. Years later, they are often left damaged or disillusioned. But whatever the case, their chances of finding suitable mates are diminished because they have spent years with "substitute" men.

What can you learn from these women? I think there are a few lessons.

Mr. Wrong can't be right

Don't waste your life with Mr. Wrong. There are far too many cases of women who were in relationships with the wrong guys during their prime dating years. In the end, they break up. In the end, they are still single, and older, yet not always wiser. It begs the question, even if Mr. Right came along during those years, would they have recognized him?

Get out while you can!

You are pretty sure he is not right for you, but you don't want to be alone so you stay with him. Staying in the wrong relationship or with the wrong man won't suddenly make it right. Don't delude yourself by thinking you can change him or that things will get better. You can probably convince yourself that he really is the right man or you can make him right. But ultimately, even if you don't get out of a relationship when you can, it will likely end anyway, one way or another. The longer you stay, the harder it is to get out — and the more significant the consequences.

The best way to avoid the trap of a dead end relationship is obvious — just don't go there in the first place, don't get involved in one. Yes, it is easier said than done. But it is a great deal harder to leave a relationship than to avoid one in the first place.

Ever wonder which men and relationships to avoid? If you're really honest with yourself, you likely know the answer. But sometimes you are afraid to trust your own instincts or you're afraid of being lonely. But the pain and damage to your self-esteem from being in a bad relationship is not worth it.

Choose wisely, avoid married men
Don't leave your good sense, judgment, standards

or your values behind when you enter into a dating relationship. If you want to get married, a man who is already married is not the best choice — not to mention the obvious conflict if you are a Christian. There are some cases where men who are separated do eventually divorce their wives and remarry. However, that seems to be the exception, not the rule. For your own sake, avoid an intimate relationship or maybe even any relationship with a man who is married or separated until he is able to give you a commitment. If he is serious, I am pretty sure he will sort out his life and come after you. If he is not, it will be pretty easy for you to figure out, whether or not it's worthwhile. In the meantime, you are still available to meet other men who are truly available to you.

Make sure the man you are dating has integrity

Integrity! I love that word. It basically describes someone who says what they mean and means what they say. I recognized this quality in my husband quite early in our relationship. When we first started dating, I knew if he agreed to do something, I could be sure it would get done. It was an attribute I found rare and almost surprising, because too many of the men I had encountered during my dating years lacked that essential quality.

Take off the blinders!

Don't let your insecurities or his "perfection" interfere with you seeing him for who he really is. If like Leah you are young, naive and unfortunately put your trust in someone who did not deserve it, don't let him steal any more of your precious time. Once you leave the relationship, do whatever you can, including getting professional help if necessary, to heal yourself from the damage caused by his failings. Let success and happiness be your goal.

Although Cassie and Leah have not met their mates yet, both still hope to get married. Both are strong, independent and successful women. One has an impressive career and enjoys traveling. The other is a successful business owner, who is raising a bright and articulate child. They did not let their lack of success in finding the right mate limit their success in other areas of their lives. And even if you share their story, neither should you let that limit your success.

> *Then there is Violet. I met Violet in my early twenties. She was a strong Christian woman with a bright future. She was in a long-term dating relationship and in her mid- to late-thirties. She was waiting for her boyfriend to be ready for marriage. From my perspective as an ob/gyn resident, and given her age, I wondered about the wisdom of her being in a lengthy relationship, without the prospect of marriage. Maybe she wouldn't be able to have kids. Eventually Violet did get married to her longtime boyfriend, waiting until she felt he was ready. She was well into her thirties when she finally got married. Despite her age, I vividly remember visiting Violet after the birth of her first child. She was right about her man and she did not wait in vain.*

Follow God's direction

If you have been dating a man for several years, or even several months, don't be afraid to objectively evaluate your relationship. If your goal is marriage and his is not, decide whether it is a good idea to stay in the relationship. If you still are not certain, consider what you want out of life and from your relationships and remain open to God's word. He will make it clear to you. The biggest problem you will face in making the decision is not knowing the right thing to do for certain, but rather listening to God and obeying His word. Don't let the fear of being alone make you stay in a bad relationship or impatience cause you to leave. Trust that you will be guided to the right decision and pray for strength and courage.

If you are not sure what Mr. Wrong looks like versus a man who is truly worth waiting for, the next chapter can provide some examples.

5

Who let the dogs out?

Some men treat women badly and develop a reputation for being "dogs." The behavior is so bad that I sometimes wonder if we are being a little unfair to man's best friend. But there are those who have exhibited somewhat "doggish" behavior, but ended up becoming pretty decent husbands. How does that happen? Well, sometimes the difference is not just how they matured over time, but in the timing of the relationship.

Some years ago, I asked a male colleague of mine what was it about his wife that made him choose her. He didn't launch into a discussion of how she was *The One*. Rather, he admitted that he had met plenty of nice girls before dating his wife, but he just was not ready. In other words, it wasn't just a matter of whether or not his wife had some special qualities, but rather that he was finally ready to commit. Those other "nice women" didn't really have a chance.

Ignore the glitz

In the dating world, all that glitters is not gold. And if it does sparkle like glitter, run in the opposite direction. By *glitz* I mean guys who you know deep down are just too good to be true. You want to believe all they say, but a nagging voice inside your head keeps sounding alarms. He may be good-looking, successful and a great conversationalist, but something just doesn't seem right. His words are sugar-coated and reassuring to your ears. He seems 'perfect' and especially good at stroking your ego. But that's because he's had a lot of practice, mostly with unsuspecting, vulnerable women. These guys know exactly what you want to hear because they are attuned to your needs and insecurities and they prey on those weaknesses. If there is a school for smooth operators, they are at the top of the class.

Often these are the guys who start talking about marriage from Day One. They tell you what a great wife you would be even before they get to know you. That is not to say that there aren't genuine guys out there who talk about marriage early on in a relationship and really mean it but with careful observation, the difference becomes clear.

But how do you recognize them? Trust your instincts and carefully observe them to see if their actions match their words. These "glitzy guys" start out really strong. But the minute a woman gets really interested, they cool off. They like to flip the script and try to make the woman become the pursuer.

Here are a few real-life examples:

When Joan met Darren she thought he was cute, but she didn't take him seriously. But one thing led to another and they started dating. Things were great for the first few weeks, but then his true colors began to show. He enjoyed hanging out during the weekdays, but was almost never around on weekends. She was always available for him, but he was seldom there for her. When she started to pull away, his calls increased. She explained her needs for more time and a stronger commitment and he made many promises, but failed to live up to them. She finally ended the relationship, but not without doing damage to her self-esteem and suffering considerable self-doubt.

More red flags:

Susan had a similar story. When she met Derrick, she thought he was attractive and a smooth talker. She was interested in dating him, but she wanted to take it slow and agreed that both could date other people — at least at first. He insisted that he was ready for a serious commitment. She complied. He talked about marriage early in the relationship. But as soon as she had committed to an exclusive relationship, she began to see signs of him wavering. He was a little less available. As she became more invested in the relationship, she unwittingly became the pursuer and he increasingly retreated from the relationship. He found ways to blame her for the problems in the relationship. She tried harder, but nothing improved his behavior. Finally, she ended the relationship, but not until after significant emotional turmoil.

Here's another example:

Gina met Greg at a nightclub. He was beautiful to look at

— *tall, dark and handsome. Even so, she knew he was wrong for her from the start. He wasn't stable and she had difficulty trusting him. Still, he was so attractive. He was the "perfect" gentleman. He opened doors and pulled out chairs and he was an excellent lover. But he drank a lot, and was drunk almost every night. The relationship ended nastily. He borrowed some money from her to pay his mortgage. She ended up getting sick and needed the money to pay her medical bills. He repaid her with a bounced check. When she got out of the hospital, he was gone. He had changed his number and she was never able to reach him. She was able to recoup half of the money she had loaned Greg from his brother. Years later she still regrets the relationship.*

What did Joan and Susan and Gina do wrong? And what is the lesson for you? They all went against their initial instincts. Joan knew that she should not have taken Darren seriously and she was right. Darren would never have lived up to her expectations.

If she had moved at a slower pace in the relationship, Susan might have realized earlier on that Derrick was wrong for her, before she became emotionally attached to him. Gina knew Greg was unstable. That fact came back to haunt her.

Trust your instincts and don't get distracted by empty promises. God gave you wisdom for a reason. Don't ignore the warning signs. You do so at your peril.

A number of women I spoke with whose marriage ended in divorce did admit that they had warning signs before the wedding but they ignored them. One woman said her friends had warned her, and that her fiancé had even broken several promises before the wedding. Another had decided to end the relationship just before she was to get married, but her fiancé promised he would change. Ultimately, he convinced her not to call it off. A decision, she lived to regret.

Tiffany learned that lesson the hard way. She wanted to get married, and live out a fantasy life replete with the white-picket fence and two or three children. She met Sam, her first husband when she was only eighteen and he was perfect on paper, or so she thought. He was educated, ambitious, bright, hardworking, cute, came from money and they had similar backgrounds, according to Tiffany. In other words, they had a lot in common. But there was another side to Sam. Early in their dating relationship, he would curse at her. Other times, he would spit on her. There were times he would stop the car they were driving and tell her to get out. So why didn't she leave? She had invested so much in the relationship and she thought that his behavior would change in time. She stayed in a relationship with him for five years, all the way to the altar. Family and friends warned her, even on the day of her wedding. She decided she'd finally had enough after eight years of marriage when her first child was still very young. It was the "last straw," she said. "He held me against the wall and was strangling me," she said, recalling what happened after one of their fights. Later, as he was sleeping, she packed a few of her things, took her child, and told him she was leaving. He barely acknowledged her. "He thought I was joking." She never returned.

So if you see these early signs, don't ignore them. Tiffany knew that Sam was abusive early on in their relationship, but she thought he would change. She ignored the advice of family and friends and pressed ahead. She overemphasized the superficial things they had in common, such as his intelligence, his work ethic and his background and minimized his disrespect of her and his abusiveness, which should have been the deal breaker.

However, you can't always avoid mistakes in life and that includes relationships. Forgive yourself for the bad choices that you have made in relationships or the red flags that you may have ignored in the men who you have dated. After all, you are only human. Learn from your mistakes and use those important lessons to make better choices about the kind of man you want to marry and those you want to avoid.

As painful as these relationship failures may have been, those experiences can be your best teachers.

6

The search for Mr. Right

If you are sure you want to get married — and hopefully you have learned some of the men to avoid — here are some suggestions as to where to meet the right man.

I first saw my husband at a neighborhood gym. I thought he was 'cute,' and although he smiled when he saw me, we never spoke. About a year and a half later, we met at a party through mutual friends. Little did I know that he not only remembered me, but had been hoping to run into me. When I first saw him, he was in a relationship, which ended long before we started to date. It explained why he hadn't pursued me at the time. When I met him, I was frustrated with dating and could have

THE SEARCH FOR MR. RIGHT

easily decided that I was going to withdraw from the social scene — but I decided against it. My advice to you as you try to find your mate: make the effort. By that I mean, continue to be socially active. Attend parties, exhibits, movies — whatever events and activities you enjoy that are part of your social life. Be open to opportunities to meet other people. Consider online dating services and other social media. A recent study found that more than one-in-three American couples met their spouses online and that those marriages are less likely to break-up and be more satisfying than those who meet off-line (at least for the first six to seven years). Regardless of how you meet your mate, you need to scrutinize them in much the same way.

I asked several women the same question — How did you meet your spouse? — and I got some interesting answers that I'd like to share. One woman told me that she met her partner while pursuing her nursing degree. She was asked out to dinner by a man that she knew. She agreed, but on one condition: that they each bring a friend. She wasn't sure of her interest in the man, so she cleverly set up a double date. Her date's friend eventually became her husband and they've been married for well over forty years. Other women met their mates through male or female friends. One woman was particularly fortunate. She met her husband of almost fifty years in the living room of her very own home. Her brother had invited him to their house; but needless to say most of us did not and will not have this kind of luck. So where do women meet their spouses:

Go out!

It's the obvious answer. It does not mean that you should go to places you don't enjoy just to meet someone. But do make an effort to participate in activities that you enjoy and try to avoid becoming a recluse. Go to that concert your friend really wants to attend, even if it's outside your comfort zone.

Jessica was not into sports, in fact she considered herself something of a non-athlete and a bookworm. Reluctantly, she accompanied her girlfriend to a game, which was how she met George. Several years later, he became her husband and they have been married for over 45 years.

Keep an open mind. You may not marry the guy you go on a blind date with, but he may become the person who introduces you to Mr. Right. Or, maybe you introduce him to a single friend of yours and they are a match. Your husband could be just another friend away.

Live! Participate in activities you enjoy and be open to new things. Don't be afraid to say hello first. Even though I believe that guys should be the ones doing the pursuing, a smile or just a hello may be all the encouragement he needs to make his move. Two women I know met their husbands after starting up a conversation with their future husbands.

We worked together

Several women have met their spouses through work. Of course, that can be a very difficult situation since some companies have policies that prohibit employees from dating. Others don't, but it may be a tense work environment if the relationship goes sour. Tread carefully, but sometimes it can be worth the risk. A useful approach in that situation may be to keep the relationship platonic and see how it develops. Hopefully the friendship will help you recognize whether the relationship is worth the career risks.

I met him through my sister
Even family members can be helpful in finding a mate. Be open to meeting people through introductions and family-related activities. Don't ignore their dating advice. After all, they know you better than most.

Childhood friendships rekindled
It sounds so romantic when you hear stories of people marrying their childhood sweethearts. But there is no certainty that those relationships will lead to a happy marriage. Therefore, apply the same level of scrutiny regardless of how long you have known him.

Met in college through mutual friends

College can be a great time to meet your spouse. It is also important, however, not to rush into marriage even after a long-term college relationship. Pamela first met Zach while she was in graduate school. He came by to borrow notes from her roommate. She went out with him for a drink, but they didn't see each other until a year later when they met again at work. They got married after three years of dating. They were married for more than thirty-five years, until he died from cancer.

An upscale jazz club

Nightclubs may not seem like a good place to meet someone, but you never know. Don't eliminate someone as a prospect just because you met them under less than ideal circumstances. After all if a nice girl like you is at the nightclub, why can't a nice guy, like your future husband, be there too? Although Emma admits that it was not always easy, she considers herself happily married to a man she met in a jazz club more that sixty-two years ago.

A wedding

My mother was only eighteen when she met my father for the first time. The sister of a mutual friend was getting married and their mutual friend innocently arranged for my dad and his friend to transport my mother and her sister to the wedding. Although they initially dated for about three years, they were then separated since both left their homes and traveled to different countries to pursue their graduate education. They saw each other on only two occasions during those seven years while they were apart.

Ten years after they first met, my father moved to New York City, where my mother was living. Within three months they were married. My parents have already celebrated forty-eight years of marriage and my mother describes her marriage as happy.

Someone from the neighborhood

Olivia and Dylan lived on the same street. She met his brother initially and some years later she met Dylan. She already knew his family and his background but then she got a chance to know what he was about. The attraction was far from intense initially, but three years later when they did get married, she had fallen in love.

Being set up on a blind date

It is not that Heather wasn't ready to meet someone, but she wasn't head-over-heels about the prospect of another blind date. She went on a date with Adrian, and although she found him interesting, the feeling did not seem to be mutual. He stopped calling her. She decided to take a chance on Peter. He seemed like a nice guy, but initially there weren't any sparks on her end. Peter on the other hand was definitely interested. He asked her out on another date almost immediately. It took her a little while, but she eventually realized the deeper feelings she was developing for him. Nineteen months later, they were married. She made sure to invite the mutual friends, who had set them up, to the wedding.

Introduction through friends

Connie went out with a group of friends one night. They brought Craig along. She and Craig started talking. And it was the beginning of their relationship. Within four months she knew he was the right man for her, and they were married within three years.

Participating in activities

"I met my husband in college," says Crystal "I was playing table tennis with his friend and he became intrigued because I was the only female in a group of males."

Candace and Mark both played badminton with different groups, and she saw him regularly on the court. She had an outgoing personality, so one day when he came without his usual group, she didn't think twice about inviting him to play with her group. Eighteen months later they were married.

At church

Many of the women I had interviewed described

meeting their spouses in church; none of them described love at first sight.

Kerry knew her husband for many years before that initial spark. Her parents were celebrating their anniversary at church, and he offered to help her take pictures. They exchanged Black-Berry pins and started communicating with each other. After her initial attraction to him, the main things that influenced her decision to marry him were their shared commitment to their respective families, their faith and their ability to move beyond their arguments.

Abigail was divorced with children and was very wary of men. Although she had known Harry since childhood, at that time, she says "she did not like him." Years later, they ended up attending the same church. A friend of hers tried to set her up with him, but she resisted. One evening she and her children sat next to him at church. One of her children fell asleep leaning against his shoulder. That innocent act led to the beginning of their relationship. Seventeen years later they are still happily married.

Met online

With the popularity of social media and online dating sites, more and more people are making connections that way. You will have to take steps to check him out, but make sure you thoroughly investigate his background.

Sean was a handsome successful doctor. You'd think it would be easy for him to meet the right woman. Not so. He met his wife through an online dating service, and he has no regrets!

You may have already met him...

The road from the first boyfriend at summer camp to husband had a lot of twists and turns for Pamela, but it led to a happy union for her.

When you least expect it

Dina met her husband Terry about fifteen years ago:

"I met my husband ... on the beach. He owned a water sports company, and I bargained for a Jet Ski ride."

Another woman met her husband by chance. They recently celebrated their eighteenth anniversary.

"We met at... a hospital, working part-time and going to school," said Jean. *"We introduced ourselves. Or I should say Fred introduced himself, and gave me his number since I*

wouldn't give him mine."

Or under unusual circumstances

The amazing thing I have discovered about how people meet their spouses is that it is often serendipitous. Many times it's when you let your guard down or when you're not really looking that he comes along. Don't worry if sparks don't initially fly, or if he does not pursue you after the first meeting. It doesn't mean that he is not the one. Even someone who vanishes from your life may come back around again. And if he doesn't, have faith that he is not The One.

Kate was a nurse and Victor was her patient. After he left the hospital they met again through mutual friends and he pursued the relationship.

Recently, a high school friend of mine shared this particularly beautiful story of how she met her husband of sixteen years.

"I met my husband in a nightclub in a town called Pinetamare, Italy. I had seen him once before, but had not seen him again until that night. I wasn't even looking for anyone. I

wasn't dressed the part. I was in no mood to be out, much less hook up with anyone. I didn't want to be there, but I promised a girlfriend that I would go out with her that night since it was her last week in Italy. I was sitting with my back to the dance floor when someone tapped me on the shoulder. I turned around and there he was.

"I immediately felt butterflies in my stomach, but I played it cool. He asked me to dance and I agreed. I gave him my phone number. Gary called the next day and I wasn't into talking. The truth was, the guy I was dating at the time, Bert was sitting across the room from me. After that I never heard from Gary, who would eventually become my husband, for a while. We've known each other for nineteen years and been married for almost sixteen. I think God gave me my husband.

"It turned out that Bert was married and he had lied to me. In addition, he had a baby with some other woman... I guess after Gary called, he decided to confess to me as a way of keeping me. (It still took him another month to do it.) We separated that night. The next night I literally cried myself to sleep. After all I was a good person and felt that I deserved someone good in my life and that is what I told God in my *prayers. I fell asleep while praying and crying. . . Sometime the next morning the phone rang and it was Gary, the guy I had met in the club a month earlier. The first thing I asked him was why he had never called me back. . .. He said that I sounded so cold over the phone and in the meantime he temporarily lost my number. . . I believe that my prayers to God were the reason that we reconnected."*

Here's some advice that should help you when you start going out and meeting men. I am a proponent of the numbers game: The more men you meet, the more likely it is that one of them will be your husband. A few more things to remember that can help you avoid some of the distress I went through — *yes, distress.* When you meet a man, you are just meeting a man. Avoid the temptation to start evaluating whether he is your future husband or not. If you find him interesting and the interest is mutual, start getting to know him better in much the same way as you would if you'd just met anyone new. If you don't like him as a friend, move on. However if you do like him as a friend, don't worry about whether you are attracted to him or whether he is husband material. Enjoy the new person in your life and build a friendship with him. If the relationship becomes romantic, meaning if he happens to express a strong interest in dating you and you are open to it — go with the flow — but only if you like the direction that the river is flowing. If you are only interested in friendship, be straightforward and let him know. If you are not interested in any relationship at all move on and try to resist the urge to dwell on the disappointment you may feel because the man you just met is not a potential mate. You will meet more guys, because you are doing what it takes to meet Mr. Right. Life is too short to spend too much time mourning what could have been instead of enjoying what is.

The interesting thing that happened when I met my husband was that although I was open to meeting new people, I did not do an immediate assessment of whether I could marry him or not. In fact, when I met him, I eliminated him as a possibility because I thought he was too young for me (my husband ages well). Thankfully I did not dismiss him. I remained open and went with the flow. It certainly did not take long for God to make it clear to me that indeed, this time I had struck gold! The experience was similar for many of the women I interviewed. Initially, they didn't necessarily see their future husband as marriage potential, but they didn't dismiss them from their lives either.

Like the saying goes, you'll likely find him when you are not looking. Before meeting my husband, I thought fat chance. I am always looking, but as my great God should have it He managed to strategically place my husband in a direction that I indeed was not looking. I am so glad He did!

7

Looking for love (in all the wrong places)

You are out and about now and you have begun meeting new guys. It's a great start. As you begin meeting all these new guys and you expand your social circle, don't be afraid to really get to know them. At first, you may want to restrict your interactions to group settings, and if you find someone who you like as a friend — setting aside your pursuit of a husband for a moment — nurture the friendship. Yes, they may develop an interest in you or you in them, but unless it is mutual don't dwell on the relationship. If he is the one who is interested in you and he has made that clear and you don't feel the same way, be honest with him. And if you are both comfortable with the relationship, allow the friendship to continue.

I have been fortunate enough to have enjoyed platonic male friendships. In some cases unrequited interest became an issue, but for many it did not. In fact, I was introduced to my husband by platonic male friends at a party we were all attending.

Male friends not only provide companionship, but can also provide much needed insight into the way men think. In some cases, as with me, they can even introduce you to your life partner.

Suppose you meet someone on a blind date or online, but you are only interested in a dating relationship. How do you handle that?

My suggestion is to keep an open mind. Don't overthink a blind date or visualize your wedding dress even before you've met him. Try to live in the moment and focus on the actual date rather than on what it could lead to. If it's a dinner date, enjoy his company, your meal and the conversation. If the experience leaves you somewhat disappointed, look for the positives and chalk it up to experience. If you both enjoyed it and want to meet again, go ahead but take it one step at a time. Avoid the temptation to think too far ahead in the relationship. Allow it to proceed naturally.

When you meet someone online, find out about him before you ever meet. However don't be lulled into a false sense of security and reveal more about yourself than you should, or reveal too much too quickly. Take your time getting to know the person you're in a relationship with and don't ignore your instincts just because you met online or on a blind date.

Not to oversimplify friendships between women and men: In many instances, one person may be interested in more than just friendship compared to the other. However, God can resolve those situations for good for those who love and serve Him, even platonic relationships that seem too complicated and difficult to navigate.

One of the biggest challenges that you may find

when you are dating is summed up in the chorus of the popular 80s song "Lookin' for Love." The point is that you may meet a guy and the attraction is mutual, so you might be tempted to overthink it. You look at the positives and try to convince yourself that you have met your future husband, and begin planning your future with him. Stop, take a deep breath, and spend some time to get to know him. Do your best to maintain your objectivity. Don't start making this new man you meet into the version of him that you would like him to be. Rather, see him for who he is and don't forget the criteria you've established for what you want in a mate. Don't forget the qualities you value most because he's interested in you. Most of all, don't be afraid to walk away. Even if the interest is mutual, that doesn't necessarily mean that the two of you are compatible. The negatives of pursuing the friendship may exceed the benefits. The same God who brought Not-Quite-Mr.-Right into your life is the same God that will bring the *right* man into your life.

Keira was introduced to Kyle by mutual friends. They were both hanging out at a café and talked for hours. The conversation was great. Despite initially hitting it off, she knew almost immediately that he wasn't right for her. She ignored the warning signs and pressed ahead with the relationship. Some of her friends convinced her that the relationship was worth pursuing, even though, deep down she knew better. She tried to make Kyle fit her ideal man instead of acknowledging that he just was not the right for her. Instead of walking away when she should have, Kyle walked away from her. She ended up suffering more than she probably would have had she trusted her intuition and moved on right away.

8

How will I know?

I love Whitney Houston's music. She was and I suspect always will be my favorite female artist. If I had a crush on anyone when I was growing up, I would ask: "How will I know?" Shortly before I met my husband, a friend of mine got married after a brief courtship. When I asked her how she knew that he was the right man she said, "You just know."

I now realize that when I asked myself that question in the past, it was because he didn't really love me. I never had to ask that question with my husband. I just knew. How did I know? Perhaps because I was ready and fully aware of the man I needed, because I knew that he was the man God was leading me to. I felt a sense of peace that I had not experienced in any of my dating relationships before meeting my husband. A friend of mine echoed a similar sentiment when asked about her husband of fifteen years. She described a "serene, calm feeling" that she experienced whenever they were together. Even though I have been married for more than ten years, I still consider myself a novice. So I decided to ask the question — *How will I know?* — to a group of women who have been happily married for at least ten years. In response, I heard a number of interesting observations from the women I interviewed.

Contrary to the 'love at first sight' romance popularized in the movies, none of the women I talked to cited that kind of fairytale love story. Some described a strong feeling of knowing — you can call it intuition — that their future husband was the right man. Some described how well they got along with their future husbands when they were dating. Others mentioned having a lot in common with their mates. Many women described the qualities that their husbands had, and how his relationship with his family was significant in influencing their decision whether he was right for them. Another reason cited by some women in determining whether he was The One was that he allowed them to be themselves, and in particular that he was not controlling.

"My spirit felt at ease at all times," said Sandra about her husband of fifteen years, which was something she needed. "He allowed me space," she said, "coming out of a claustrophobic relationship." A few divorced women who I interviewed complained of a controlling spouse, which was one of the reasons for the demise of their marriage.

When will I know?

You won't necessarily know whether he's Mr. Right after only a few dates, a few weeks or even months. Sometimes it takes years. An old classmate of mine admitted that although she ended up marrying her first boyfriend, it was years after their teenage relationship had ended and she had refused his proposal several times that she finally agreed to marry him.

Chantal met her husband of more than twenty years when she was only eighteen. He was only one of several male friends she had in college. Since she was focused on her studies, it took a while for her to realize he was interested in her. "Once I figured it out, I told him that he should pretend like he didn't know me in school. I wasn't sure if I was all that interested and wasn't prepared to take the teasing from my friends unless it was worth it!" Her more mature self is still surprised that her younger self did that.

A former colleague of mine admitted that her husband had been interested in her and had proposed marriage for years — she had turned him down repeatedly — before she ever considered him marriage material.

Ultimately, the question still remains. What's important in helping you decide if the man who you are dating should be your husband? Here's some good advice from the women I interviewed that can help you answer the question: How will I know?

I. **First and foremost, do not rush into making a decision.**

Yes, it is possible to recognize Mr. Right. But be sure that you are not acting out on an emotional impulse, or as one woman put it, in a "love cloud." Yes being in love is a great feeling, but that is all it is — a feeling. It can generate a sense of euphoria — an incredible high. But just like any other drug, you don't want to make life-changing decisions when you are under the influence. The feeling of being in love is not the only thing that may make you rush into a decision. Some women are concerned about their biological clocks. Others may let pressure from their potential spouse cause them to rush their decision. For example:

Chloe fell in love with Matthew. She thought that he was the right person and would fulfill a need in her. But then she started to notice something about him. She saw a jealous and controlling side. She began to have doubts about the relationship and was planning to leave. However she allowed Matthew to convince her to stay. She married him within ten months of their initial meeting. She stayed with him for 15 years and it took another four years before her divorce was final. She regrets that she did not take the time to know Matthew better. His controlling and abusive behavior took a lot out of her. She advises women to take the time to get to know who their potential spouse is and that they should not be pushed into a marriage.

If you feel swept up in the decision to get married for whatever reason, listen to your inner still small voice and if it says Wait, obey it.

2. **Observe him in different situations and see how he treats people.**

   This point goes back to liking the person. Do you really like the person he is or just the way he makes you feel?

3. **Date for at least one year.**

People can change and act differently over time. Obviously, I did not obey this suggestion since I married Ryan within four months of our engagement and less than a year after our first conversation. But I certainly think this advice can be helpful for many people.

4. **Marry someone who you feel can be your best friend, because in the end that is what will keep you together.**

I always had a best friend. In fact she was the same person from my late high school years, throughout college and into my professional life. It was always an extremely important relationship. At times she was the person I shared the most with. Something changed after my marriage. We still had a strong friendship but the person I needed to talk to every day was no longer her, it was my husband. He had become my best friend without me even thinking about it. What I can say is that I knew I liked him before I knew I loved him.

5. **Seriously think about your decision.**

   You can't jump in and out of marriage. You should know enough about him that you want to stick around. Even though getting a divorce can be easier than it was in the past, it can still exact a high personal and financial toll.

6. **Beware of red flags.**

   Many divorced women admit that they saw the red flags and chose to ignore them. One woman explained that she chose to ignore warning signs, because the wedding plans were so far along.

   Heidi met Kent at a bachelor party. She reluctantly accompanied a girlfriend who was invited. They were only in the same country for six months of their fifteen month courtship but she fell in love. Their romance was full of adventure and travel and she knew she would never have a boring life with him. Still she had her doubts but she ignored it. Her friends tried to warn her but she blocked out their advice in the same way that she blocked out the negatives that she noticed about

Kent. He broke his promises. He even broke one on the eve of their wedding. Nevertheless, she married him anyway. It only took one year for the happiness to fade. The divorce was complete five years later.

Let Heidi's mistake be a lesson to you. Those red flags are God trying to warn you. But like so many other things in life, we sometimes choose to ignore Him at our peril. Remember, you have an out, all the way to the altar when you say I do (and even after). Hopefully, if you choose to end the relationship, you do so before the wedding ceremony. In the long run, it is the best timing. Don't let your decision be clouded by concerns about the money you've already spent on the wedding, the opinions of others or your desire to get married. Rather, base your decision on the two people who are most important at that time: you and your potential husband. Calling off the wedding if you know you should is the most loving decision that you can make for both of you.

7. **Try to look beyond the moment and choose someone who you can grow old with.**

   We can't see the future, but forget about love for a moment and ask yourself do you really like him enough to spend the rest of your life with him?

8. **Know the man and his family, because you will be a member of that family.**

   Both my husband's parents are deceased. Someone said to me, I was lucky that I did not have to deal with in-laws. Clearly, the comment was coming from a lot of pain that person endured because of their in-laws. Do your best to start off the relationship with your husband's family on the right foot. If the relationship with your in-laws doesn't seem to be working out despite your best efforts, create the appropriate boundaries between you and your in-laws needed to sustain your relationship.

9. **Take your heart out of it and use your head.**
   Alyssa had a very intense physical attraction to Xavier. The way

he made her feel convinced her that she wanted to spend the rest of her life with him. She ended their dating relationship when she discovered that he was living with his first wife after he had told her that he was living with his mother. But she took him back. She ignored the fact that he had made several promises but never followed through and used the excuse that he did not have the money. She ignored the red flags because she allowed her feelings that he was her soul mate to cloud her decisions, blinding her to everything else. Eventually they got married. But his dishonesty took a toll on the marriage and the relationship and she too became a victim of his infidelity. The marriage lasted eight years. Her marriage to him taught her that love should be based on honesty and respect and her decision to spend the rest of her life with a man should not be based on just sexual chemistry.

Being in love is a wonderful feeling. It is intoxicating. Don't make such serious commitment based on your love-struck heart, but rather use your God-given brain.

10. Make sure that the person you marry has similar interests and beliefs.

Not all your interest and beliefs will be shared,

but I certainly agree that it is good to have enough in common so that your interactions are not a constant battle of wills. For example, if you do not share the same religious faith, you may face conflicts in the way you live and how you choose to raise your children.

II. Never settle!

Don't marry a man who you are not convinced is the right choice for you out of fear that you won't get married. You're underestimating the power of God. "…If you abide in me, and my words abide in you, ask whatever you wish and it will be done for you." John 15:7, *English Standard Version*.

To paraphrase some of the encouraging words of Joel Osteen, keep the faith, God has big plans for you and that includes a great husband if that is His calling for you. So don't settle for Mr. Ok instead of waiting for Mr. Oh Yay!!!!

12. **Find a man who loves God and treats his mother and other women with respect.**

    There's a saying that goes, a man will treat his wife the way he treats his mother. I've never had the privilege of meeting my mother-in-law, but I have always heard that my husband was very close to her. I certainly feel that he honors her in the way he treats me.

13. **Good communication is essential.**

    My husband and I were attending Mass one day when the priest asked a question that he poses to couples: what is the most important thing in a marriage? Both my husband and I believe the answer is *communication*. I think the ability to express your thoughts and feelings is essential to any healthy relationship. The absence of good communication in a marriage can make or break a relationship.

14. **Discuss things such as finances, how to raise children and discipline.**

I will mention this a little later in the book, but discussing issues such as your potential husband's credit history, how he handles his financial obligations and his view on spanking children, for example, are important because big differences can lead to significant discord in a marriage

15. If someone shows you who they are, believe them.

In a psychology course that I completed, I learned that we all have an idea of who our perfect mate is and we compare the person we marry to that ideal. When you are in love, you run the risk of minimizing or overlooking certain flaws. And while it is healthy to see your spouse in the best light, when you are dating it's unlikely to be in your best interest to not recognize the person you are dating for who they really are. No one is perfect and neither is your prospective husband, but be certain that you love him in spite of his shortcomings and vice versa.

16. If a man has "baggage," don't ignore it. Observe how he handles it.

Whenever you are on a plane, the flight attendant asks you to make sure that your baggage is properly stowed and secured in the overhead bins. If not, that baggage can wreak havoc when you open up the overhead bin. Make sure you talk to him about the steps he plans to take to handle his baggage — with his exes, with his responsibility to his children if any, with family or business obligations — to avoid having the baggage smack you in the face.

17. Any faults he has will multiply ten times over. Flaws only get worse, so don't think that you can change him.

Before you marry him, you should know your future husband's faults and be willing to accept them. That's not to say those flaws won't still be annoying after you are married. But if you are aware of them, they won't be a deal breaker.

18. To live, or not live with him — that's the question.

Whether or not you should live with someone before marriage is debatable. However, among the women I spoke to, many of those who lived with their spouse before marriage ultimately ended up divorced. One recurring theme for some of these women is that when they decided to live together before they made the decision to marry, marriage seemed like the "right" thing to do.

Bianca lived with Cory for seven of the eight years that they dated prior to marriage. She cared about Corey a great deal and maybe even loved him. But that is not why she married him. She admitted that she was bored with her relationship and considered leaving him but since they were living together and since he was a "nice guy" she decided to "hurry up" and get married before she changed her mind. Her marriage lasted for less than one year.

On the other hand, I know a lovely Christian woman who I knew many years ago decided to live with her fiancé a few months prior to the wedding to save money. Some research has suggested that couples who live together are more likely to divorce. But other studies suggest that the age at which couples decide to live together correlates better with a successful marriage, when couples choose to live together before getting married. Sometimes, if the decision to marry precedes a couples' decision to live together, it seems that the odds of the marriage working out seem to be better than if the decision to marry comes after they decide to live together. This is backed up by research. Furthermore living with one's partner before the marriage is neither a license nor an obligation to be sexually intimate if celibacy is your goal but it could increase the temptation. I think that ultimately your decision whether or not to live with your partner should not be based on society's opinion, but rather on God's guidance. However be well informed of the facts of your decision and recognize that living with a man before marriage rather than being good preparation can be a set up for failure. Having accurate knowledge combined with prayer and biblical teaching will help you to better distinguish your will from God's will.

Know him well

Like Tiffany, of "the white picket fence and two or three children," many of us make the mistake of dating or even marrying men based on our perception of who they are or who we think they could become. Unfortunately, they do not usually become the men we hope they will be, but rather the men who they have always been. It is possible for a man to have a life-changing experience and become the man who you hoped he would be. But don't count on it. And if he actually is a changed man and he believes you are that someone, allow him to come back to you. But don't wait around for him.

And yes, at the end of the day it is still a risk. Hopefully, your decision is one that is informed by good judgment, and, if you rely on God — prayer. Many of the women I spoke to who held a strong belief in God felt it was important to make Him the center of the marriage.

Here is an example of a calculated risk:

Victoria met Glen at a party she attended with her girlfriend. She was only twenty years old at the time. She found Glen attractive, but he was of a different race and from a different country, which was thousands of miles away. Five years later, she married him and returned with him to his home country. She candidly admitted, "I was taking a hell of a chance, but I knew him [very] well and loved him." She has been happily married to her husband for almost fifty years. Perhaps what was most important to the success of her marriage was in what she said: [she] knew him very well. Her decision to get married was guided by knowledge, and not just love.

Sometimes the right man comes along in a package you would never have dreamed of. Do you remember Pamela and Zach?

Pamela thought Zach was gorgeous, intelligent and thoughtful. But, there was a but. She was in her twenties and he was thirteen years her senior. He was from another country, divorced with three kids. But she did not allow her thoughts to be clouded by his good looks or to be daunted by his baggage. He did not fit the image of Mr. Right, but she recognized they had a lot in common, saw his good qualities and realized that he was worth the risk. Despite the real and sometimes very difficult challenges they faced, she loved being loved by him. She appreciated his affection, their love life, his knowledge, the fact that they never ran out of things to talk about, and the fact that he became her best friend. Even after their more than thirty-five-year marriage, which ended when he died, she was glad that she was the one that he spent the rest of his life with.

If you meet a man whom you believe could be the right man, but you are still not sure, my advice to you is, wait. Avoid the temptation to rush into a relationship or marriage. Pray and be open to God's guidance, even if it means walking away. I am confident when I say that if you keep praying and maintain open lines of communication with God, He will make it clear. It is your responsibility to listen to Him. If you listen to Him, even if things don't work out as you had hoped, believe that they will work out for the best.

9

The wait is over

You have finally met him! Alleluia and amen! You may have felt so frustrated and filled with doubt that you didn't dare even hope this day would ever come, but too afraid to believe that it would not. Even if you are as sure as you have ever been about him and have no doubt in your mind, you should still seek premarital counseling. One of the best places to get counseling is through your local church. The church that my husband and I got married in required us to take premarital classes. I won't pretend that I remember too many specifics of each session but I have no doubt that those sessions strengthened our marriage. For us, it also began our relationship with our parish priest, Father Michael.

He was instrumental in many aspects of our life including the baptism of our children and much needed spiritual advice on major life decisions.

Premarital counseling can help you to identify and discuss issues that you may have overlooked. It can provide a safe environment to broach topics that you may have been afraid to discuss. It can provide reinforcement for your decision to marry or give you pause in forging ahead with marriage, in some cases.

In preparing for marriage, there are a number of subjects that you should discuss, especially if you have not talked about them or you haven't come to some resolution.

I.   Decide whether or not you want children. How many and are you open to adoption?

2.   Where do you want to live? What city or what country if that is relevant? Would either of you be willing to move from where you are now to someplace else and under what circumstances? Would you be willing to live

apart if that becomes necessary?

3. What religion do you want to raise your children? Do you want to raise them in the church, and if so what faith? What denomination?

4. Discuss each of your personal and professional goals and aspirations. Of course, they may change but you don't want to blindside your partner with information that either of you knew even before entering the marriage.

5. What kind of role do you want your in-laws to play in your marriage, and are there any unresolved problems with your respective families currently? Be diplomatic in this discussion; they will be your relatives too!

6. Have an open and honest discussion about your finances, including the debt that each of you will be bringing into the relationship. Discuss your credit history, your income and any other significant financial matters.

Finances can have significant implications when you get married and are one of the biggest reasons for arguments in a marriage. In fact, studies show that disagreements about finances are one of the issues most likely to cause couples to divorce.

7. Be sure to talk about sex. It is entirely up to a woman to decide how much of her sexually history she wants to reveal. However, I do think it is important for both parties to reveal whether or not they have had sex before. Personally, I think the number of sexual partners you have had in the past is irrelevant. But both you and your partner should get appropriate screening for sexually transmitted infections and be up front about them. I think couples should talk about their preference regarding the frequency of sex and what kind of sexual experimentation is desirable.

This list is by no means exhaustive, but it provides a start. Counseling will give you a framework for discussing more topics that are important to a successful marriage. If there is ever a time to talk about these issues, it is at this point in your relationship, before you take your vows — even if it results in you changing your mind. As hard as it may seem to end an engagement, it doesn't come close to the pain of ending a marriage.

10

Ryan and Me

As I write this chapter, I remember the first time I saw Ryan, my husband of more than ten years now. (I didn't notice him at the time, but he noticed me I later learned.) It was at a holiday party at a difficult time during my single years.

In 2003, I was celebrating yet another Christmas holiday season as a single woman. I was contemplating whether to return home to the lush hilly suburbs of Kingston, Jamaica, where I was raised, to be closer to my family. My parents had taken me there from New York, where I was born, when I was only ten months old. I remained in Jamaica throughout high school but left there at age 17, to go to college in the States. And although I frequently returned home, I spent most of my adult life in the US. I dreaded the thought of being a single woman in a place like Jamaica, where everyone over 30 seemed to be married. My two closest friends from high school, both physicians like myself, who had remained in Jamaica, were married with children.

I was living in Silver Spring, Maryland, at that time, on the border of Washington, DC. I was generally happy with my life. I had completed my residency at Georgetown University Medical Center and had been working for more than three years. I even spent two years at a hospital in Florida, but returned to the DC area, because, frankly, it was the place where I enjoyed my single life the most. I had lots of friends who were single. We always did things together, everything from bike-riding to rock-climbing, to parties at each other's homes or at nightclubs. But something was still missing. I doubted that I would meet someone in Jamaica, but I felt a strong urge to return to the place where I had grown up.

A few months earlier, I had met someone in

DC who I thought was a great guy. I met him at a summer party hosted by mutual friends. Initially, it seemed that the feeling was mutual, and for a short time we were dating exclusively. But a few months into our relationship, he (I'll call him Mark) told me that he would prefer if we just remained friends. I was disappointed and it was painful. He was aware that I was considering leaving the DC area, and returning to Jamaica to be close to my family — a decision that would make a serious relationship between us impossible. He encouraged me to stay in DC, at least until the following summer since my plan was to move during the winter. But I wasn't prepared to remain in DC just to spend the summer with someone who had already decided he did not want to pursue a relationship with me.

That December 2003, fifteen years after I moved to the US, I went back to Jamaica for the holidays as planned. One of the reasons for returning to Jamaica was to decide whether to return home for good. I was at a holiday party at the home of a close family friend. I was with my parents, and my brother and his wife. It was a small party with about 20 or 30 guests. The party was outdoors, one of the luxuries of winters in Jamaica. The setting was beautiful, surrounded by lush vegetation and nearby hills. There was another couple at the party, and I recognized the woman from high school. They looked really happy, standing slightly apart from the crowd. Watching them only intensified my loneliness. I was sure that everyone at the party was happily coupled except me.

Two months later, I moved back home to Jamaica, for good. I settled in to a quiet life in a suburb of Kingston.

About one month later, I was at the gym and I noticed a handsome, well-built man. He had the physique of a body builder, and was about average height. One thing I remember was that he had a pleasant smile. He had short-cropped, dark brown hair, and dark brown eyes. I did not realize it at the time, but he was the same man from the holiday party, who was one half of the couple I'd wistfully admired. He smiled when we exchanged glances, but nothing more.

I didn't see him again until a year and a half later. It was another holiday season, and I was feeling the disappointment of another year of dating futility. It was only a few days before Christmas, but despite my mood I was determined to enjoy myself. I attended an all-inclusive party, a signature of Jamaican parties. For a fee, you can enjoy an outdoor party with all the food and drinks included. Since Jamaican social circles are fairly exclusive, I was sure some of my friends and acquaintances would also be attending the party. One of the organizers was the brother of one of my closest friends, who I knew would be home with her husband and children. There were a few hundred people, including many singles and couples. At the party, Ryan and I were introduced by mutual friends. It was our first formal introduction, and thinking back, it was pretty unremarkable. I didn't even get his name right. "You said your name is Brian?" I asked.

"No, Ryan," he replied. He spent the remainder of the evening talking to me. I remember little about our conversation, but I was struck by the fact that he gave me his undivided attention.

That night, Ryan walked me to my car and we exchanged numbers. He promised to call me. Having heard similar promises and been disappointed before, I wasn't sure what to expect. After the party, my girlfriend asked me about him. I said I thought he was too young for me. (Actually, Ryan is two years older than me, but he has aged well). To my surprise, he did call and immediately asked me out.

On our first date, he took me to a Japanese restaurant. I was surprised and impressed, since it was an unusual choice for a Jamaican man. The conversation was easy, and I felt comfortable and relaxed.

Even though we had only met a few days before Christmas, Ryan asked me out again for New Year's Eve. I wasn't sure, but I liked his company and I was happy to have a date for that night, especially since a few weeks earlier I was sure I would spend the night alone.

On New Year's Day, Ryan took me to dinner, where I met many members of his extended family. I guess I should have felt overwhelmed, but I didn't. I just went with the flow, much like my Auntie Monica had years ago. Over the next month, we talked on the phone every day, and saw each other almost as much.

By then, I was certain he was the right man for me. It was almost inexplicable. I felt a kind of peace and calm you feel when you've made a decision that you are confident about. It wasn't a decision based on feelings or emotions. It was based, in part, on knowing how the right man was supposed to treat me. Unlike other times in my life, I didn't have to question God or ask anyone else if they thought Ryan was right for me. I think God spoke directly to my soul.

There were other things, unusual things that

happened, that made me believe that this time —
that he — was different. For some reason, every
time Ryan kissed me, my nose turned red. It was
almost comical as I think back on how it happened
again and again while we were dating.

Later, when we compared notes, Ryan said he had
also known it. He admitted that he remembered
seeing me at the holiday party almost two years
before we were introduced, and at the gym. But he
was in a relationship at the time. He read an article
about me in the local newspaper, a month or two
after we'd exchanged looks at the gym. After his
girlfriend ended their relationship, he kept an eye
out for me at parties that he thought I would have
been likely to attend. He did see me at one party,
but I was with a male friend, so he assumed that
we were dating. He did not see me again until six
months later, at the party where a mutual friend
had introduced us.

As I reflect on the first time Ryan noticed me,
until we started dating, I cannot help but think that

sometimes we meet our life partners, but things don't work out because of timing. It doesn't mean that we weren't meant to be, but sometimes it requires coincidence and circumstance, and patience.

By May of 2006, less than six months after we had started dating, Ryan and I began talking about marriage. By July, we were engaged.

Ryan's proposal was unique. Since he was an avid scuba diver, early on in our relationship he had encouraged me to learn to scuba dive. I took lessons, because it was something that was important to him, so it was important to me. By the summer, I had almost completed my certification and was ready for a sea dive. We went away to the seaside town of Portland, where Ryan grew up . It is one of the most beautiful parishes in Jamaica and the location of numerous screen productions, including scenes from the movie Cocktail with Tom Cruise. We stayed with a relative of his. One day, we went diving. I noticed on the boat ride out to the dive spot, he kept asking the boatman about the visibility in the water. I didn't think too much of it at the time. We went down into the water. We were 43-feet below sea level when I noticed the large sign planted in the water. It said, 'Monique will you marry me?' I nodded yes. He even had a ring that he called the honorary substitute ring, which he placed on my finger. When we returned to land, I called my parents who already knew he was going to propose, since he had asked their permission to marry me. Afterwards, Ryan and I met his brother and sister in-law, who were also in on the proposal that weekend, and who had planned a lovely meal at a local restaurant. On the return trip to my parents' home we started planning our wedding. We were married in November of that year. Frankly, we could have married sooner, but we both wanted a big wedding. There was never any doubt. We were both sure of each other.

Like any other couple, over the past ten years we have had our ups and downs. We have moved five times, including moving to the United States, where we currently live and are raising our children. We have two beautiful children, Zane and Kia, and over the years have had some financial challenges. However, if we had to do if all over again, we would still make the same choice.

My advice to anyone who wants to find The One: be open to new opportunities. Be open to meeting new people, and allow their actions to speak louder than their words. And trust that your God, our God, has got this too!

11

Let's talk about sex

Salt-N-Pepa's song was a hit with me like it was with so many people. At the time, I was more focused on the catchy lyrics and the beat. Now, however, I realize it was part of an important social commentary. It described a woman who could have sex with any man she wanted to, have all the material things her heart desired, but she was still unhappy. It spoke to the dangers of unprotected sex and highlighted the distinction between having sex and making love. That distinction is something that is central in the struggle of a Christian woman grappling with her sexuality.

Like me, many girls growing up have felt a commitment to the teachings of the church regarding avoiding pre-marital sex. Let's face it, there doesn't seem to be much ambiguity about premarital sex in the Bible. It is clearly against it.

> Marriage is to be held in honor among all, and the marriage bed is to be undefiled; for fornicators and adulterers God will judge.
>
> Hebrews 13:4, *American Standard Version*

However, in the 21st century you'd be hard pressed to find many women abstaining from pre-marital sex. The question is why and what happened along the way?

From a practical point of view, I suspect it is much easier to remain celibate for five or ten years than for fifteen or twenty years. Consequently, a woman who gets married in her early twenties would have had a greater chance of honoring that commitment than someone who doesn't get married until her late thirties, forties or older. Despite the challenges, there are women who have maintained their virginity into their late thirties and even forties.

But it is much more complex than that. A woman's ability to maintain her vow of celibacy is likely affected by many factors including her personal resolve and commitment to the vow, her self-esteem and the kind of relationship she has and the type of men she dates. As far as men are concerned, it can get tricky because the man you are dating may not share your views. I think you owe it to yourself and him to be honest about your commitment. It will help weed out the guys who are only there for the sex and those who stick around for the long haul. It will let you evaluate your feelings more clearly without sex clouding your emotions.

If you decide that it's important to maintain your virginity for marriage and do so, I congratulate you. If you have not been successful, but want to renew your commitment to abstinence or even if you want a reason why abstinence might be worth it in a world where sex is such a dominant force, read on. Toni, Celia, Wanda and Chelsea have shared extremely valuable insights into the importance of pre-marital celibacy for women in the success of their marriage.

Toni married her husband Clarke when she was twenty nine. She had already lost her virginity in her early twenties. Although she admits that she wanted to be a virgin before marriage, she was not "devastated" by the fact that she was not one. She admits that she did not have a strategy to maintain her virginity, but her family upbringing and other interests saved her from battling with the decision until her twenties. At the time she was fine with her decision, but she was conflicted. She struggled with society's influence perpetuated in the media, peer pressure and even some family members made her feel that it was normal to have pre-marital sex in contrast to her religious beliefs that it was a sin. Even now, more than ten years into a happy marriage, she admits that she regrets having sex with "the losers" she met and got involved with before marriage. She also said that if she had maintained her virginity, she would not have had to struggle with the guilt of having sinned and the fear of sexually transmitted infections. Toni acknowledges that they are many forces that will determine the outcome of one's marriage. Now, as a parent, she believes that she can prepare her children as well as she can, and leave the rest to God.

There are other reasons women chose to remain celibate before marriage:

Celia is a thirty four year old virgin. Her mother's admonition that she should remain a virgin is the primary reason she has remained celibate, she admits. But when she became a Christian at age fifteen, her commitment became personal. She made a vow to keep herself for her husband and to honor God. She has had to be proactive to maintain her celibacy. She avoids compromising situations. She avoids going to her dates' homes or inviting them to her house. She eliminates temptation in the form of books, movies and conversation. She even memorizes Scripture to fortify her resolve.

Celia believes that when she does marry, there will be a host of benefits to maintaining her virginity. "I won't have the memory of past experiences impacting on my new experience with my husband.... not bringing the memories of good or bad," she says, to the marriage bed. "I will be free in an undefiled setting to create wonderful memories with my husband. I won't worry about passing on sexually transmitted infections to my husband, or fretting about whether or not I'm pregnant from last night's exploits. I can stand before him knowing that he alone will 'know' me."

She does admit to some disadvantages, such as being ridiculed by her peers, the fear of pain and discomfort when she eventually does consummate the marriage — given her lack of experience. Ultimately, she has no regrets. Her advice: "If one is a committed Christian, the ability to wait is symbolic in that it shows your trust in God to keep His promise of providing a mate for you. I am aware that effort is involved in making a marriage work. I'm aware that I have to bring more to the table than just my chastity. But that's a step towards being obedient and committed to Christ. This must count for something in my relationship with Christ and eventually my husband."

For some women, abstinence is a part of a strict upbringing:

Wanda was able to maintain her virginity for thirty-eight and a half years, until she got married. Although she admits that it was not always easy, her success was influenced by a few factors. She was raised in the church and she strongly believed that her body was a "temple of God" and that she "should not defile it." She was also extremely close to her mother and was highly influenced by her. Her mother had taught her to value her virginity and to maintain it until marriage and she wanted to make her mother proud. Fear played a minor role in maintaining her celibacy. She was afraid that if she had sex, her mother would somehow find out. She was afraid of pregnancy and the potential adverse effect on her career. She admits that the men she dated respected her decision, although they certainly tried to convince her otherwise.

Wanda is proud that she maintained her virginity until marriage. When she did marry, she was guilt-free and she avoided any sexually transmitted diseases.

She candidly admits, however, that there is a downside. She says that sex was painful at first. She believes that it would have been less painful if she had married at a younger age, but that was beyond her control. Her strong religious "rigid" upbringing inhibited her comfort with sexual experimentation with her spouse, such as trying new positions. She did not feel prepared for sex prior to marriage since the church's position on premarital sex was abstinence. She tried to prepare herself by watching pornographic movies, but she realized that these movies were "perverted" and could not help her learn how to enjoy sex. She feels that sex isn't all that it's cracked up to be, and she admits that she lacks the knowledge and sexual experience to achieve an orgasm.

Still, she is glad that she waited, but she still wishes that she had gotten married at a younger age.

Circumstances can also influence one's decision about premarital sex:

Chelsea had a strong faith and commitment in God from her childhood days. She had strong positive influences and attended church with her grandmothers, her parents or on her own. She had a strong conviction, even in those early days, to maintain her virginity. Before she entered her teens, something changed. A close relative began to sexually molest her. She became confused and felt trapped in a situation that felt terribly wrong. She felt dirty, her purity stolen. Although she was molested, she was still a virgin. But she felt that her chastity was compromised. After all, she was "no longer pure." She did not lose her virginity until her early twenties and it was within the confines of a loving relationship. However, her self-esteem was further damaged, because she had now willfully broken her promise to God.

The molestation had an even more detrimental effect on her future relationships. Chelsea realized that it was still her choice whether to have sex or not, but several years later she believes that this experience affected her ability to trust that God would help guide her choices about her sexuality. Now Chelsea is happily married, and while she still wishes she had not experienced sexual abuse and has had to struggle with forgiving herself for some of the choices she subsequently made, she is confident in the promise that "all things work together for good for those who love God who are called according to his purpose." (Romans 8:28, *New English Translation*)

Whether or not to maintain your virginity before marriage is a choice for some, but not for everyone. For those of you who were denied the choice, God does not judge you based on other people's sins. If it has led you to sexually promiscuous behavior, know that He takes your circumstances into account. Either way, His forgiveness is always available. For those of you who are not virgins and live with regret, forgive yourself for any poor choices that you may have made and though it may be incredibly hard, try to forgive those for the choices that were made for you. The process of learning to forgive under situations such as rape and childhood sexual abuse may take years of counseling but it will be worth it. For those who have made choices that you are happy with, thank God for his strength and guidance. And for those who have made choices you regret, thank Him for the wonderful ways He will turn your experiences for the good.

Depending on whether or not you or your husband is a virgin, you may still have a lot to learn about each other sexually after you walk down the aisle. Keep yourself open and be a willing and eager student to fully enjoy this God-given gift in the context in which He meant it, within marriage. Yes, sometimes it may be difficult after years of abstinence or even years of teachings about the evils of premarital sex to become a fully sexual being, but those sexual urges were instilled in you by God because He knows its value within the context of a healthy marital relationship. But He also knows the harm it can cause under the wrong circumstances. Use the gift of your sexuality wisely.

12

What about love?

I grew up in Jamaica where I was raised Roman Catholic and attended a Catholic elementary school. I remember at quite an early age being asked to read I Corinthians 13. The version I read was from the Good News Bible, *Today's English Version* a Protestant version of the Bible that was sometimes used in my school.

> *"Love is patient and kind; it is not jealous or conceited or proud, love is not ill-mannered or selfish or irritable; love does not keep a record of wrongs; love is not happy with evil but happy with the truth. Love never gives up: and its faith hope and patience never fail. Love is eternal. . .Meanwhile these three remain: faith, hope and love and the greatest of these is love."*

It was and still is one of my favorite passages from the Bible. So at an early age I was exposed to, in my opinion, one of greatest descriptions of love ever written.

However, I have always been a hopeless romantic. Cinderella is my favorite fairytale, and I doubt there is a romantic comedy or cinematic love story that I do not like. So it was from popular movies that I formed my ideas about being "in love." I thought that I was in love if I had an intense physical attraction to someone — a sense of euphoria when I was with him. But that feeling came with anxiety and depression if I did not see him or at least hear from him. Of course, I wanted to be with him all the time and I had butterflies when he was around. I almost did not dare to be my true self, because I wanted to receive his love in return. The worst part of believing that this was how it was supposed to be "in love" was the certainty that I had — at least in my twenties — that this feeling was necessary before determining if someone was the right person for me.

After I met my husband and realized he was

right for me, I learned a different kind of love. Yes, I enjoyed seeing him a lot and I appreciated the time I spent with him. But I did not experience the anxiety and pain associated with it. I was not anxious when he did not call; but he always called.

It is often said that love is not enough, but I am convinced that the problem is not with love. Maybe the problem lies with how we define and express it. But it's more than that, though. I have also learned that the feeling of "being in love" is not even required for someone to have a long, successful, happy marriage. Unlike those movies that lead us to believe otherwise, it takes more than just chemistry to make a marriage work. On the contrary, it may actually lead us to the wrong choice in choosing a mate.

In trying to understand how emotions play into relationships, I asked women — both married and divorced — if they were in love when they got married, and how they defined being in love. For those who were still married, I also asked them if they were still "in love" with their husbands.

Many women, both those who remained married and those who did not, described being "in love" with their husband when they got married. For most of the women I talked to, their definition was that romantic kind of love, "butterflies and all." Almost without exception, those who remained happily married for several years had a new definition of being in love, which had little to do with the romantic love of their youth.

One woman described it this way: "Now it is a quiet dependence. We read each other minds, look out for each other. I look out for him and he for me."

Another woman described it this way: "This is someone you love and care about and you don't want anything to happen to him."

However, there was a key difference between many of those women who were "in love" and stayed married versus those who did not. Many women whose marriage ultimately ended in divorce, married while they were swept up in the "euphoria" of being in love — often after an intense initial attraction. That wonderful feeling allowed them to commit, despite the presence of some huge "red flags." In some cases, they considered themselves happily married for years. However, when the feeling of infatuation faded, they saw more clearly that it takes more than butterflies to sustain a marriage. They realized that the men they had chosen would never fulfill the needs required for a long-term relationship.

On the other hand, many of the women, who remained married, got to know their spouses before they fell in love. This provided them an important perspective on the man that they were actually falling in love with.

A dear friend and colleague summed it up beautifully. She has been happily married to her husband for almost forty years. Although she recognized that he was her husband from the first time she met him, she readily admits that she was not "in love" with her husband when they got married. And although she was confident in her choice, she actually grew to love him.

What she learned, however, was a beautiful definition of being "in love." She defined it as a deep caring and respect for her husband. So much so, she said that even if her husband left her for another woman and he became ill and needed someone to care for him, she would want to be that someone — no matter what. Because of the great love that they had shared, she would want to be the one there for him when he needed someone the most.

The final piece of advice in determining whether or not the man is right for you comes from her: "Let the butterflies go" before you make a decision to marry the person, so that you know if he truly is the person you really want to marry.

In other words, don't let infatuation or that chemistry you feel being "in love" cloud your judgment. Make sure that your decision in choosing the right mate is based on reality and not an illusion.

13

Don't let him slip away

During my dating years, one of my dear friends shared her insights about marriage, which she believed to be true — the kind of conventional wisdom that make women panic and worry about their biological clock. She maintained that if a woman was not married by age 35, it was because the opportunity had passed her by. I was rapidly approaching that age at the time and even after thinking about it long and hard, I did not feel that I had missed the "right" man, but I decided to examine the question for this book.

I spoke with a number of single women — aged forty and older — and without exception, they all thought that they had missed an opportunity at marriage. However, this "unwritten rule" is not true for all women. I will share some of their stories.

Kelly met Jim when she was in her early twenties. She knew he was the right guy, but at the time she did not feel comfortable attending a particular church with him. Ultimately, she ended the relationship. She believes that if she stuck to it, maybe she might have ended up marrying him. Years later he married another woman, and he and his wife are not members of that church.

Here's another example:

Sandy met Godfrey when they were in high school. She was only fourteen at the time, and they dated for three years. Although they were very young, they both knew they were right for each other. However, he went away to college and although he wanted to continue the relationship, she felt the need to explore other relationships. Ultimately it ended. Later, she tried to rekindle the relationship, but he was so hurt by her decision to pursue other relationships that he refused. He also ended up marrying someone else.

More examples that love has no timetable:

Bill was Sarah's best friend since she was fifteen. He was handsome, and she admitted, a decent person. When they were approaching age thirty, he asked her to marry him. She said no. Years later, she still grapples with trying to understand why she turned down his proposal.

Or an 'ideal' match:

Julie knew that Mark was interested in her, but he was of a different race and she was a little older than he was. She did not allow the relationship to progress. He eventually got married to someone who looked a lot like her.

Or the 'perfect' situation:

Katy has decided that she no longer wants to get married. She is in her forties and she does not want to burden a spouse with the ongoing medical issues that she faces. But there was a time when she did want to get married. She knew Adrian loved her. Adrian wanted to marry her when she was in her twenties, but she did not want to be "tied down." Even now she knows that he is the kind of man who would have taken care of her in her illness, but it is too late; he married someone else. She still wishes that she had settled down with her "first love."

Although some of these women had reasons for avoiding marriage, many of those reasons did not stand the test of time and their decisions have sometimes left them with regret. Obviously none of us can see the future, and we should be guided by what we think is the best decision at the time. Do your best to ensure that the decision is based on the right reasons.

This time I am never going to let you go

It may help if you re-evaluate your checklist of qualities you want in a mate and consider only those that are most important. Carefully contemplate what factors you are willing to compromise on, and let go of those hang-ups that may be impeding your success in choosing the right person.

You can't recapture time lost, but you can learn from experience so that you don't miss your next opportunity.

Elizabeth knew that she had made a mistake when she let Richard walk out of her life. She had to wait more than fifteen years before another opportunity came along in Charles. Although she'd had some difficult relationships in those fifteen years, she also benefitted from a great deal of soul-searching and spiritual growth. So she was ready when Charles came along, even though he exhibited some of the same "over-eagerness" in pursuing the relationship that had made her run away from Richard. Since then, she had grown enough to recognize the good man that Charles was and to be comfortable enough to follow his lead. They married within one year of their first date.

If you let the first Mr. Right walk out of your life, forgive yourself and move on. Become the person who you want to be. Participate in activities that you enjoy and keep an open mind. When the next Mr. Right comes into your life, you want to be ready and willing to take the plunge.

So get ready, suit up and dive in!

14

I'd rather be alone than be unhappy

I doubt that the many little girls who grow up wanting to get married and have the dream of a nice house with a white picket fence and two or three children running around ever think about divorce as being part of that picture.

Ending a relationship is never easy. So for those who have never been through it, it is hard to imagine the pain of divorce. As a Catholic, I was taught that divorce was not an option. My mother is a non-Catholic Christian so I was also familiar with some of the protestant teachings on divorce. One passage that I was familiar with during my childhood years was as follows:

"I tell you, then, that any man who divorces his
wife for any cause other than her unfaithful-
ness, commits adultery if he marries some other
woman." Matthew 19:9, *Good News Bible*

Then I grew up... not to say that I no longer
believe in the teachings. I do. But I realize that
sometimes one's commitment to marriage may not
be authentic or fully realized by both people. What
may have been true for one may not have been true
for another. One party may have meant their vows
and the other party may have been deceptive.

When I started interviewing divorced women
for this book and I asked them their reasons for
getting divorced, several answered infidelity. I made
the assumption that of course infidelity was reason
enough and there was no need to delve further into
their reasons for divorce. However, when I read
through their answers and talked to more divorced
women, I realized there was more to it. The reason that many women leave their marriage despite
sharing children with their spouse is complicated.

And for many, infidelity is often only part of the problem.

"The worst part of it," says Ginger, married for thirty-one years before she divorced her husband, "is the feeling of being trapped in the relationship. It takes a big chunk [of you] emotionally. And on [one's] self-esteem, it can be very destructive."

Ginger's thoughts were echoed by many divorced women.

After ending her marriage of seven years, leaving her a single mother of two young children, Carly, recalls that it is so easy to get into, but so hard to get out of. The worst parts of staying in her marriage were the sense that she could not get out and the guilt associated with ending her marriage and accepting that it had failed.

But both Ginger and Carly did get out, and Ginger admitted to having more peace in her divorce than she did in her last twenty years of marriage.

Simone married Bill when she was twenty-nine years old. She was in love, but admits she made fundamental mistakes in her decision to marry him. She wanted the relationship to progress to a sexually intimate level. Because of her faith, she wanted that sexual intimacy to be within the confines of marriage. Simone brought her then-boyfriend to church since she was becoming seriously interested in him, but was advised against using that as reason to bring him into the church. Even her pastor advised her against marrying Bill. But, she was in love. She valued her Christian faith and she wanted Bill. So against the advice of her spiritual advisers, she married him. She even expedited her wedding date to accommodate an extended period of travel that she had previously planned to take because she was afraid he would be gone when she returned from her trip.

She was enamored with him for the first five years of their marriage, but then her first child came. He became jealous of the time that she spent with their daughter and left her with the bulk of the financial and parental responsibilities. He was often missing. She was no longer the happy person that she was or the one that she wanted to be. "I was crying all the time. I stuck with it because I wanted to honor my commitment and because I was in the church." Her breaking point came when one Christmas morning their child asked for a bicycle that her daddy had promised her. She questioned him about it and he admitted he made the promise, but he said that he did not have the time to fulfill it. "He could have asked me. I was mad, I did not buy his excuse, and I decided then and there that I was not doing this every Christmas." She found out later that he had another child during the marriage but she insists that was not the issue. Her divorce was finalized seventeen years after she first married. She has realized forgiveness was important especially for the sake of the children, who maintain a good relationship with their father and each other.

In another case:

Stacey married her high school sweetheart, Shane, but she knew even before the wedding that the marriage was not meant to be. They met each other when they were only twelve-years-old and she fell in love with the sweet boy that he was. She noticed a change in him after his parents divorced, when he was sixteen. But she still loved him and she desperately wanted him to succeed. Even from that time she "was always doing stuff for him" including his homework. She sincerely thought that she was helping him. Stacey got pregnant with his child when she was nineteen years old. They remained together for two years and then she ended the relationship but they reunited two years later and there was a second pregnancy. She married him after only a few months to "honor her faith". He was repeatedly unfaithful to her and

*he "relived everything" that "he hated about his own father".
She hoped and believed he would change but it did not happen.
It started to affect her health and even her relationship with her
God because she felt that she had to stay in a marriage that she
should not have entered in the first place.*

*So one day she left. They were married for six and a half
years. She left for her health, she left for her children and she
left for her faith. It has been two years and she still loves him
but realizes very clearly that she did not put him in his proper
place. Her love for him was "borderline idolatry" . . . and he
was a "god for her."*

Stacey has learned many lessons. She now knows
what she deserves and she understands her worth.
I believe these lessons will help her choose a suitable mate should she so desire, and help her to be
a better mother for her children.

I have chosen to write this book from a woman's perspective, and as such I have only interviewed women; but I will make one exception. I
have a baby brother. He is far from a baby right
now as he is in his forties but even now, I still

refer to him as my baby brother. As a big sister I have always been protective of him, something I have in common with my older brother.

My youngest brother divorced for reasons that most people, arguably, would agree were justified. It was not easy for him, and as his sister I hated to see him suffer and experience such betrayal. However, there was a question I asked him that I also asked many of the divorced women I spoke to. Were there any red flags? His answer, years after the divorce, is still the same. No. This chapter is also for those women, like my brother, who just didn't know. They genuinely thought they knew the man they had married, but found out he wasn't the person they thought he was. Some may feel betrayed, even duped. Some may just be angry... angry at themselves, angry at some of those close to them for not noticing — perhaps even angry at God.

Forgive yourself. Forgive those you love and even the person who you hold responsible, even though you may feel that you hate him right now. Stay close to your God, and carry on with hope and courage. Your past, by no means, has to determine your future. Like childbirth, sometimes the greatest joy comes after enduring great pain.

For me, Abigail's story is a message of hope.

When she was only eighteen, Abigail married her first husband, Justin. She met him at church. Even though Justin was ten years older, she was very much in love with him. She "worshipped the ground that he walked on." In retrospect she realized that part of her willingness to enter into the relationship was influenced by her wanting to escape a very strict household. She had to grow up quickly in the marriage. She had to be a mother to her stepchild and quickly had two other children of her own. She felt trapped and became very unhappy in the relationship and at times wanted to run away. She realized that she did not want to be controlled and hated the fussing and arguing. After eight years of marriage she decided to leave.

Today, after seventeen years of marriage to Harry, Abigail says she is happily married. She had not expected Harry to be the one, but he exceeded her expectations. She has a marriage in which she and her husband complement and respect each other. She has found a man who is a "great person" and "a wonderful father to her kids," a man who she is able to "trust with her life" and who has proven himself over and over again and that he is still there for her. She says she doesn't know what she would do without him. She has discovered a love borne out of a deep trust.

Do you wonder what ever happened to Tiffany? Well, she did learn from her hard lesson in love. Although she paid a high price, she was able to walk away from her verbally and physically abusive husband. She did not look back. Looking forward allowed her to meet Conrad. He was not going to enter her heart easily. She now had high standards for a husband and she was not going to repeat her past mistakes. Conrad did not fit her traditional definition of the ideal man. He was many years older than her and he had children from his prior marriage but there was something different about him. Contrary to Sam, Conrad embraced all of her family members "black sheep" included. Something that was particularly important to her since she cared about family. Unlike Sam, Conrad made her a priority and continues to do so. They share mutual interests, something that was also lacking in her marriage with Sam. She and Conrad attend church regularly together while Sam may have talked the talk about being a Christian but never walked the walk. Tiffany is now happily married to Conrad and she believes that God in His wisdom knew what she needed and wanted in a partner and sent Conrad to her.

By no means do I think that any woman or man, for that matter, should feel trapped in a marriage. I think the decision to stay or leave should be based on prayer and guidance from God. You may get advice from family and friends, but be very discerning about whom that advice comes from. Although many people mean well, their advice is sometimes more harmful than helpful. Know that you have a God of second chances — and sometimes third, fourth and fifth — and trust that even if you have to walk away from your marriage, He will lead you to a brighter future than you could have imagined possible. If you doubt it, remember Abigail and Tiffany! As for my baby brother, God did not forget him. He too is now happily remarried and he and his wife have a beautiful daughter together. I am confident in saying that my brother has gained more than he ever lost.

15

And they lived happily ever after

As a child, my favorite fairytale was Cinderella. For as long as I can remember, I have always been interested in relationships — how they work and the ingredients of a long-lasting one. During my years as a single woman, I often asked married women how they met their husbands and what the initial attraction was. I was interested in finding out what the keys to a successful marriage are and the formula to avoid divorce.

Since I enjoy romantic movies, I would even try to analyze them and noticed that some of the greatest love stories ended too quickly for one reason or another: The Titanic, Love Story or Bridges of Madison County for example. It left me to wonder, does the kind of love depicted in the movies really exist? I was all but convinced that that was the kind of love I needed when I met The One — the kind of love that sweeps you off your feet. But does that kind of love really last? There may not be a secret formula for a long-lasting, happy marriage, but there are some lessons to be learned from those who have succeeded.

This is Karen's story:

"My husband was my high school sweetheart. I met him through a friend when I was sixteen-years-old and going to . . . high school. I was in grade eleven . . .at the time. We shared the same circle of friends and so we would hang out together all the time. We have been together for twenty-six years and ... we celebrated our twenty-first wedding anniversary last year. I got pregnant when I was eighteen-years old and my family was disappointed. They were adamant that we should get married because of our Christian beliefs. It was a difficult time for me as young as I was. Although we loved each other, we decided that we were not going to get married because of a child. We married two years later . . . when I knew for sure that there was no pressure and that this was the man I wanted to spend my life with. Our son . . . was our ring bearer."

". . . I wouldn't say our marriage is flawless, because we have had our ups and downs. I do know, however, that there is nobody else in this world that would love me the way my husband loves me. Indeed, I love him too and we continue to share happy moments together. I pray that the bond that we share will never be broken and we will be together for many, many, many more years to come. . .."

So how does any marriage survive? A long, happy marriage does not mean one devoid of hardships. There are women who have stayed married to their husbands for more than thirty years who have had to survive infidelity, alcoholism, and mental illness. But at the end of the day, they deemed their marriage a success. They did not define success as perfection, because in reality none of us leads perfect lives, but rather a marriage in which the benefits outweigh the difficulties.

Betty was married for fifty four years when her husband passed away. She says that she was a happily married woman and if she had to live her life over, she would still marry the same man. But Daniel "liked the girls" as she put it. She acknowledged that when she discovered the infidelity she cried. He apologized and tried to comfort her. She admitted that there was a breach of trust and at the time it was her commitment and her children that kept her in the relationship. She chose, however, to forgive him because he still upheld the responsibilities that she considered important in a marriage. She realized that she was not perfect and on balance, the good outweighed the bad. She also stressed that in the relationship she was "allowed to do her own thing" and he was very supportive of her.

For women whose spouses have been unfaithful, but choose to forgive and stay in the marriage, Betty has this advice: Don't delve into the details of the affair or try to investigate, because it is much harder to forgive and forget.

Fran was married for forty-seven years when her husband passed away. She too had to deal with his infidelity, but she stayed because he fulfilled his responsibilities, duties and otherwise respected her. She didn't probe into his infidelity. And even when it was brought to her attention by others, she ignored it. But she didn't shrink away in self-pity, rather she used used the opportunity for self-improvement and to find additional sources of income. She positioned herself so that the decision to stay was her choice and not her circumstance. Like Betty, Fran's husband allowed her to be independent. "He never questioned where I was going or who I was going with." Throughout the marriage, he also helped provide her with opportunities to pursue further education, even if it meant being the primary caregiver for their children when she was a student.

Ultimately, a good marriage should be based on trust.

Marci was happily married to Isaac for fifty seven years before he died. He was the only man she ever dated, however she never felt like she missed out by not dating other men. She was very confident in his love for her. She discourages women from following their partner or having anyone keep an eye on them. She did not worry about infidelity, because she trusted her husband. She based her relationship on trust. She also stressed the importance of a woman maintaining her financial independence in the relationship. She felt it important for a woman to be able to contribute financially to a marriage but to also maintain her own personal finances for anything she deems necessary.

But it is not just the big things that can cause problems in a marriage. It can be the day-to-day annoyances, like the husband who tunes out his wife when he chooses, or the husband who is always late when his wife is always on time, or the messy wife and the tidy husband.

Jessica, the non-athlete and bookworm who has been happily married to George for more than forty five years told me that George sometimes tunes her out when he wants to, and if he is busy doing something he doesn't hear her when she talks to him. Some of the differences are annoying, but she has learned to tolerate it. One example is his lack of punctuality. He is always late. To solve the problem, she has decided to either tell him an earlier time for the event or they drive separately.

Marriage involves a lot of compromise. Remember Angela who was popular with the guys but married Duane after only seven months? She was only twenty-five when she got married. Despite a very happy marriage, she admits that it has involved compromise and that she has had to give up a lot. She even admits that she may have lost a little of herself along the way. But she chose to remain married and it has paid off.

So what can women do to make their marriage last?

Some of the best advice about marriage comes from women who have succeeded in their relationships long-term:

Emma met Kurt in that upscale jazz club in London. She has been happily married for sixty two years. She advises women to keep an open mind when they enter marriage and maintain an easy-going manner — adding that patience can help a lot.

Aileen met her husband Ernie when she was only sixteen. It was not love at first sight for her. It took nine years from the time she met him until the time they married, but she was very much in love when she married him and she is still in love now thirty- four years later.

However, Aileen's definition of being in love has changed over the years. It involves understanding, commitment, compatibility and give and take. She believes communication and understanding are the keys to the success of her thirty-four year marriage. But as the mother of two, she reminds other married women to consider that they still have a husband, especially once the children come. She and her husband made time for each other–going to dinner as a couple — even when their children were small.

Paula met Ty when she was twenty three years old. She too admits that it was not love at first sight but even though she was not interested initially, six months later she had fallen in love.

After thirty years of marriage she is able to quickly say that if she could live her life over she would still marry the same man. Her advice? She recommends that women should never withhold sex as punishment in a relationship. She encourages women to be sexually uninhibited in their marriage. She advises married women to "honor their commitment. "Never take it for granted." She recognizes that marriage is an ongoing effort.

Jessica, whose husband George tunes her out, stresses that in a marriage, you can't always hold out for what is right — sometimes you have to compromise. She recognized that she and her husband have both learned to accept each other's faults. She has realized that some of her husband's faults that she was annoyed by early in her marriage were not that important. She and her husband George made a pact of never going to bed angry, and it has contributed to the success of their marriage.

And the reward?

The greatest reward for most of the happily married women that I interviewed was companionship. Simple things like having someone to go to bed with at night, the comfort of having someone to share everything with — the ups and downs, the triumphs and challenges. Here are some of the other rewards of being happily married:

"Emotional security..."

"Feeling like I have this one person, who is a constant and puts me before anything else and makes me feel safe and loved."

"Always having someone you can depend and rely on."

"It is comforting when life is hard to have someone on your side."

"Having that constant in your life..."

"Always having someone who has your back and loves you regardless of how you look or what you have done, and always knowing that someone is there."

"Ultimate definition of having a partner..."

"The sharing and benefit of raising a family together..."

"Knowing that one person who means almost the whole world to you and you to them — it is a privilege."

Here's some advice to help make your love story really come true:

View your husband in a positive light

I'm sometimes skeptical when I hear someone seem what I consider overly complimentary of their spouse. However, women who constantly complain about their husbands can sometimes be a little annoying to listen to and can also seem quite unhappy. The couples who compliment one another more seem to be on to something because if couples view each other positively, it leads to more satisfaction in their marriage and the increased satisfaction leads to increase in positive views of one's spouse.

Make sex a priority

The notion that a couple's sex life after marriage declines has often been widely parodied in movies with the familiar excuse of the wife having a headache to avoid sex. For the most part, sex is seen as more important to the man than the woman. However, that's not always the case. Having a good sex life not only improves the quality of one's marriage, but leads to a more stable marriage for both husbands and wives.

But how do you achieve a good sex life? Whether or not you or your spouse was a virgin before getting married does not guarantee that the sex will be great. Continue the discussion about sex with your partner that you started when you were dating. This time is fine to have the conversation late at night with soft music. If you feel you lack the knowledge and experience, there are many excellent books on the subject. Discover or rediscover your sexuality together. If you have any doubt that God gave you your sexuality to share with your spouse in marriage, read the Song of Solomon, in the Bible, any version. Even after you do have kids, don't ignore your sex life. You can make plans with your spouse days in advance. Sex is great exercise. It's a stress reliever. It boosts your immunity, decreases you husband's risk of heart attack and prostate cancer, lowers your risk of incontinence and that's just the tip of the iceberg. Furthermore, the more sex you have with your spouse, the more sex you will want to have. The best part is that within the confines of marriage, sex is endorsed by God. Why waste this amazing gift!

Do things together to keep the marriage interesting

My parents were friends of a wonderful couple. By all accounts, this couple had a strong marriage. They had both excelled in their careers, which allowed them the resources to travel. They owned a timeshare and used it to travel to many exciting locations in the U.S. and around the world. My parents were fortunate enough to travel with them to a few of those places, locations I am pretty sure they would never have visited if it weren't for this couple. They have both passed away, only about a year apart after many years of marriage. I did not know it then, but now I realize that these trips very likely contributed to the strength of their marriage and to the strength of my parents' marriage as well.

Couples who participate in exciting activities have better relationships. This does not have to involve costly travel; even short inexpensive activities can make a difference.

Have an attitude of gratitude

Many of us were taught common courtesies such as saying 'please' and 'thank you' as a part of our upbringing. Sometimes in the hustle and bustle of life we forget to include those basic manners in our daily life and even less in our married life. However, it turns out that feeling appreciated and being appreciative are important ingredients in a healthy happy marriage. If people feel more appreciated by their partners, they are more appreciative of their partners, more responsive to their partners needs and more committed to the relationship.

Hannah is an inspiration to me on many levels and I am truly happy to know her.

She was born with a congenital defect, non-functioning legs, which required that they be amputated above the knee, and was abandoned by her parents in the hospital as a baby and raised in foster care. Today, Hannah is a distinguished person in her community and was an accomplished athlete and the winner of Olympic medals, including two golds and one silver.

Marriage may not have been her first priority but it is something that she did think about and discussed with friends. She recognized that her disability could be a disadvantage, but she refused to allow it to be the only thing that defined her. She met Ethan when she was in her twenties. He was tall, handsome and well built. He was her roommate's boyfriend's best friend. He made several visits to her apartment after that initial visit and she wondered about his motive. It was her roommate who pointed out "he is coming to see you." They became friends, but the relationship was platonic. It took her almost twenty years for her to realize that he was the man for her. They were happily married for fourteen years until he died. She loved him for the caring and thoughtful man that he was. She loved him because he respected her and saw her for who she was despite her disability. She loved him because she felt completely comfortable to be herself with him. Although he was introverted and she was extroverted, he allowed her to pursue the things she enjoyed and she did the same. For her, the best part of marriage was having the companionship of a good friend that blossomed into a marriage. She misses the little things he would do for her. She misses the weekly Friday night movies they shared, even though she did not always like his choices. She misses her friend, she misses her companion.

Marriage is not always easy, but a good marriage is certainly worth the effort. Nurture your marriage in the same way you would nurture anything that you love. Don't take it for granted that just because you found and married the "right" man, your relationship is guaranteed to last. We are capable of making decisions that can ruin even God-blessed unions. If your marriage is failing and needs help, get counseling and don't wait until it's too late. I strongly believe that many failed marriages, need not have failed. They just did not receive the attention they needed in time.

Yes, I adore a love story and when you meet and marry the right man you can have that love story too. But there is certainly no template for happily-ever-after, not even for Cinderella. You create your own love story, and with God's help you can experience the very best love story that He intended for you.

16

It will be sooo good!

I can never forget you! I have written your name
on the palms of my hands.
Isaiah 49:16, *Good News Translation*

Laura is a sweet thirty-one-year-old woman. She
is truly frustrated being single and recently ended
a relationship with a man she loved because she
knew it was not going to lead to marriage. She
asked me, why are other women her age married
with kids and not her?

The answer, I believe, leads back to God. God
in His infinite wisdom knows the right time and
the right circumstances for each of us. Perhaps it
is not your time for marriage because He wants
you to discover hidden talents that He has given

to you. Perhaps now is the time that He wants you to cultivate your friendships. Perhaps now is the time He wants you to provide service to your church. Perhaps now is the time He wants you to provide service to your community. Perhaps now is the time He wants you to excel in your career. Perhaps now is the time He wants you to learn to love yourself and recognize what you truly deserve in a husband.

Sometimes we rush His timing and it may lead us to pain and divorce. Sometimes we miss His timing and it may lead to loneliness and discontent. Sometimes even after prayer and consideration we are led to a choice that still does not turn out the way we expected, or wanted, it to. Fortunately, He is a God of second chances. When we do find the right man it is often not easy. Some women can handle the challenges even if it hits them in their early twenties. Some need a few more years to be able to deal with them. But for those who have made the right choice, they are able to look back on their life and say like Pamela, Jane, Betty and all the wonderful women who shared their stories with me: If you could live your life over, would you still marry the same man? And the answer is: Oh yes!

My answer to you, sweet Laura and to you my dear reader is to continue to hope, trust and pray. So that when he is sent to you, you will be ready and it will be sooo good!!

Bibliography

i.   Parker, H.A. (2013). Social Support, Coping and Health. [Power Point Slides]. Retrieved from "Psychology of Close Relationships" course iSite: **http:// isites.harvard.edu/icb/icb.do**

ii.   Cacioppa, J.T., Cacioppo, S., Gonzaga, G. C., Ogburn, E. L.VanderWeele, T.J. (2013), "Marital satisfaction and break-ups differ across on-line and off-line meeting venues," Proceedings of the National Academy of Sciences, Volume 110 issue 25, June 2013, pages 10135-10140

iii.   Jeffrey Dew, Sonya Britt and Sandra Huston, "Examining the Relationship Between Financial Issues and Divorce," Family Relations, Volume 61, Issue 4, October 2012, pages 615-628.

iv.   Luo, S., Zhang, G., Watson, D., Snider, A. G. (2010). "Using cross-sectional couple data to disentangle the causality between positive partner perceptions and marital satisfaction," Journal of Research in Personality, Volume 44, Issue 5, October 2010, pages 665-668.

v. Yeh, H.C., Lorenz, F.O., Wickrama, K.A.S., Conger, R.D., & Elder, G.H. (2006) "Relationships Among Sexual Satisfaction, Marital Quality, and Marital Instability at Midlife," Journal of Family Psychology, Volume 20, Issue 2, June 2006, pages 339–343.

vi. Aron, A., Norman, C.C., Aron, E.N., McKenna, C. & Heyman, R.E. (2000) "Couples' shared participation in novel and arousing activities and experienced relationship quality," Journal of Personality and Social Psychology, Volume 78, Issue 2, February 2000, pages 273-284.

vii. Gordon, A.M., Impett, E.A., Kogan, A., Oveis, C., Keltner, D. (2012). "To Have and to Hold: Gratitude promotes relationship maintenance in intimate bonds," Journal of Personality and Social Psychology, Volume 103, Issue 2, August 2012, pages 257–274.

www.ingramcontent.com/pod-product-compliance
Lightning Source LLC
Chambersburg PA
CBHW060041030426
42334CB00019B/2438